PHYSICS IN OUR WORLD

ATOMS and MATERIALS

Kyle Kirkland, Ph.D.

Facts On File
An imprint of Infobase Publishing

This book is dedicated to Clay Kirkland,
who has devoted his life to learning and teaching.
The world could use a lot more just like him.

ATOMS AND MATERIALS

Copyright © 2007 by Kyle Kirkland, Ph.D.

Facts On File, Inc.
An imprint of Infobase Publishing
132 West 31st Street
New York NY 10001

ISBN-10: 0-8160-6115-7
ISBN-13: 978-0-8160-6115-0

Library of Congress Cataloging-in-Publication Data

Kirkland, Kyle.
    Atoms and Materials / Kyle Kirkland.
       p. cm.—(Physics in our world)
    Includes bibliographical references and index.
    ISBN 0-8160-6115-7
1. Atoms. 2. Materials. I. Title.
    QC173.K459 2007
    539.7—dc22   2006018649

Text design and composition by Kerry Casey
Illustrations by Richard Garratt
Cover printed by Coral Graphics Services, Inc.
Book printed by Maple Press, York, PA
Date printed: February, 2010

Printed in the United States of America

10 9 8 7 6 5 4 3 2

This book is printed on acid-free paper.

⚛ CONTENTS ⚛

✵ PREFACE ✵

THE NUCLEAR BOMBS that ended World War II in 1945 were a convincing and frightening demonstration of the power of physics. A product of some of the best scientific minds in the world, the nuclear explosions devastated the Japanese cities of Hiroshima and Nagasaki, forcing Japan into an unconditional surrender. But even though the atomic bomb was the most dramatic example, physics and physicists made their presence felt throughout World War II. From dam-breaking bombs that skipped along the water to submerged mines that exploded when they magnetically sensed the presence of a ship's hull, the war was as much a scientific struggle as anything else.

World War II convinced everyone, including skeptical military leaders, that physics is an essential science. Yet the reach of this subject extends far beyond military applications. The principles of physics affect every part of the world and touch on all aspects of people's lives. Hurricanes, lightning, automobile engines, eyeglasses, skyscrapers, footballs, and even the way people walk and run must follow the dictates of scientific laws.

The relevance of physics in everyday life has often been overshadowed by topics such as nuclear weapons or the latest theories of how the universe began. Physics in Our World is a set of volumes that aims to explore the whole spectrum of applications, describing how physics influences technology and society, as well as helping people understand the nature and behavior of the universe and all its many interacting parts. The set covers the major branches of physics and includes the following titles:

◆ *Force and Motion*

◆ *Electricity and Magnetism*

- *Time and Thermodynamics*
- *Light and Optics*
- *Atoms and Materials*
- *Particles and the Universe*

Each volume explains the basic concepts of the subject and then discusses a variety of applications in which these concepts apply. Although physics is a mathematical subject, the focus of these books is on the ideas rather than the mathematics. Only simple equations are included. The reader does not need any special knowledge of mathematics, although an understanding of elementary algebra would be helpful in a few cases. The number of possible topics for each volume is practically limitless, but there is only room for a sample; regrettably, interesting applications had to be omitted. But each volume in the set explores a wide range of material, and all volumes contain a further reading and Web sites section that lists a selection of books and Web sites for continued exploration. This selection is also only a sample, offering suggestions of the many exploration opportunities available.

I was once at a conference in which a young student asked a group of professors whether he needed the latest edition of a physics textbook. One professor replied no, because the principles of physics "have not changed in years." This is true for the most part, but it is a testament to the power of physics. Another testament to physics is the astounding number of applications relying on these principles—and these applications continue to expand and change at an exceptionally rapid pace. Steam engines have yielded to the powerful internal combustion engines of race cars and fighter jets, and telephone wires are in the process of yielding to fiber optics, satellite communication, and cell phones. The goal of these books is to encourage the reader to see the relevance of physics in all directions and in every endeavor, at the present time as well as in the past and in the years to come.

✵ ACKNOWLEDGMENTS ✵

THANKS GO TO my teachers, many of whom did their best to put up with me and my undisciplined ways. Special thanks go to Drs. George Gerstein, Larry Palmer, and Stanley Schmidt for helping me find my way when I got lost. I also much appreciate the contributions of Jodie Rhodes, who helped launch this project; executive editor Frank K. Darmstadt and the editorial team at Facts On File, Inc., who pushed it along; and the many scientists, educators, and writers who provided some of their time and insight. Thanks most of all go to Elizabeth Kirkland, a super mom with extraordinary powers and a gift for using them wisely.

✵ Introduction ✵

JET AIRPLANES MADE their first appearance during World War II (1939–1945), almost 40 years after American inventors Orville and Wilbur Wright built and flew the first airplane. Although jet engines are powerful and efficient, early airplanes had to settle for slow, cumbersome propellers, driven by piston engines quite similar to automobile motors. The reason that jets failed to appear first is interesting and was not due to a lack of knowledge. Engineers knew about jets all along and even had a few examples in nature to study, such as squid, which propel themselves in the sea by using water jets. The reason it took so long to build jets was that people lacked the proper materials.

Ever since Democritus of ancient Greece proposed that all matter is made up of tiny particles, people have wondered how bits of matter interact and combine. An understanding of how matter behaves gives people a satisfying explanation for many of the materials of the world, as well as the ability to construct new ones. Jet engines, for instance, burn fuel continuously and become extremely hot during operation. This heat would melt most materials, so for a long time there was no way to build a functional jet engine. Then scientists discovered mixtures of metals that can withstand exceptionally high temperatures. These materials made jet engines possible.

Atoms and Materials is a book about matter at its most basic level—*atoms* and their components—but also about how people use material in technology and society. Material exists on widely different scales, from beams of particles to slabs of concrete, and all these materials are important for a variety of reasons. On a small scale, doctors use machines that send tiny particles crashing into a cancer patient's body, hoping to destroy the disease, and engineers unleash the astounding amounts of energy in the *nucleus* of the atom to generate electricity or to make the most fearsome weapons that have ever existed.

On a larger scale, matter exists as a firm *solid,* a sloshing *liquid,* a wispy *gas,* or a *plasma* (a gas whose particles are electrically charged). Materials make transitions between these different *states,* each of which is important. Oxygen is a gas at room temperature and has a number of uses, especially relating to its roles in combustion (burning) and in life. But when people need to transport oxygen from one place to another, hauling a gas would be inefficient because gases take up a lot of space. Cooling oxygen into a liquid makes a denser cargo that is less expensive to move.

Transitions are particularly crucial in life's most important material of all, H_2O, which exists on the planet as liquid water, solid ice and snow, and gaseous vapor. The distribution of H_2O is critical to all living organisms, and an understanding of this vital substance is necessary in the conservation of the planet's resources as well as the attempt to nudge nature into giving up more—seeding clouds and making rain, for instance.

As people's knowledge of matter grows, so do the number of materials. Metals saw early uses as swords, coins, and later, airplanes. The 20th century witnessed several new materials: *plastic* that is versatile enough to find use in everything from containers to automobiles, fibers that are strong enough to make bulletproof vests, and combinations of materials that offer the advantages of both wrapped up in a single package. Perhaps the most impressive use of materials is in structures. Early houses made of wood or stone gave way to the towering skyscrapers of today, held up by a skeleton of steel. But even these buildings are mere anthills compared to plans for raising a "space elevator," a tower with a height of 62,000 miles (100,000 km) by which satellites and astronauts can reach space.

But the space elevator exists only in the minds and dreams of a few engineers at the present time, for the same reason that jet engines lagged behind their propeller cousins—lack of an affordable material with the necessary properties of strength and light weight. Materials, or a lack thereof, are critical factors in determining what gets built. The world is filled with material, each composed of some combination of the fundamental *elements*. As people continue to increase their understanding of these substances, even faster engines and taller towers will become possible.

1

ATOMIC AND MOLECULAR PHYSICS

S CIENTISTS TEND TO believe only in what they can see and experience. Yet scientists started believing in atoms even though no one had ever seen one.

Atoms made their presence felt in other ways. *Compounds* are made up of some combination of elements, and matter at its most basic level is composed of tiny particles. British scientist John Dalton (1766–1844) and other chemists and physicists who studied matter proposed that each fundamental chemical element corresponded to a specific particle. Because these bits of matter seemed to be the smallest possible pieces—thought to be unbreakable—they were called atoms, after the Greek word *atomos,* meaning *indivisible.*

Atoms proved to be real, and as instruments and measurements improved, scientists soon discovered many things about atoms, including the fact that they are not actually indivisible. Physics has taken people on many fantastic voyages into the atomic realm: Atoms are composed of even smaller particles that can be made into highly useful beams, and atoms can be split to form vast amounts of energy that have been used for both constructive and destructive purposes. The miniature world of atoms and *molecules* is still not completely understood but its importance is growing as technology reaches increasingly smaller sizes. Today physicists can even compose an image of an atom.

Seeing Atoms: Scanning Tunneling Microscope

Objects are visible because they either emit light or reflect light that was emitted by some other source. These are the only ways that objects can be seen by ordinary light. Atoms are too small to emit or reflect much light by themselves, and even the most powerful microscopes that use light cannot bring them into focus. The size of atoms is usually measured in nanometers (nm); a nanometer is a billionth of a meter and equal to about 0.0000000394 inches. A carbon atom is 0.000000006 inches or 0.15 nanometers in diameter, so small that millions would fit on the tip of a pencil. Atoms are identified by the number of particles called *protons* in their nucleus; each kind of atom is an element. The sidebar "Periodic Table of the Elements" provides more information on elements.

The instrument, called scanning tunneling microscope (STM), can detect individual atoms but it does not use light. The STM has an extremely small needle-like probe that is placed almost against the surface of the material being studied, but it does not touch the surface, as shown on page 4. The tip of the probe is so small and sharp that there is only a single atom or two at its point. The probe conducts electricity, which is an important part of the instrument's operation. As the probe moves along, a small *voltage* is applied and *electrons* jump between the surface and the probe. Electrons are negatively charged particles, and as described in a later section are components of atoms. When electrons are in motion they constitute an electric current, whether the motion occurs in a copper wire (as it does in the familiar circuits of a house) or between a sharp probe and the surface of a material. This current can be precisely measured.

How do the electrons jump between the probe and surface? Since the probe is not touching the surface there is a small gap between the two. The gap is remarkably small: It would take about 100,000 of them to equal the thickness of a sheet of paper. Even so, it is a barrier to the flow of charges. If the applied voltage was large then electrons would be thrown across and a spark would result, similar to what happens when 20,000 volts are applied across the gap in an automobile spark plug. But this would ruin delicate materials, so in the STM the voltage is small and no spark

Periodic Table of the Elements

In the late 18th and early 19th centuries, scientists noticed that a few substances seemed to be the most basic building blocks of every other material—all compounds and mixtures were composed of these basic substances, which were called elements. Scientists also noticed that elements could be grouped based on their properties. Some elements are solids at room temperature, others are gases or liquids. Some elements, like hydrogen, tend to react violently with other chemicals and some elements, like nitrogen, are more stable. In 1868, Russian chemist Dmitri Ivanovich Mendeleyev (1834–1907) discovered a way to order the elements such that they formed a table, with elements having similar properties forming columns. A number of important properties, such as a tendency to react in a specific way to other elements, showed up periodically as one moved across the rows of the table. Mendeleyev drew up a table of all 62 of the then known elements. This is the periodic table of the elements. (See "The Periodic Table of the Elements" on page 139.)

Mendeleyev's table gave order to what was otherwise a seemingly random set of elements that make up the world. The table also allowed Mendeleyev to make important predictions. There were gaps in the table and Mendeleyev predicted the existence of elements, then unknown, that should exist in those spots and possess the corresponding properties of their columns. Mendeleyev proved to be correct. He predicted the existence of the element germanium, for instance, which was found in 1886.

The number of elements has since grown to 116. Ninety of them are found in nature, and the remaining elements generally exist only when they are briefly made in laboratory experiments or in a supernova (an explosive event that occurs in some large stars at the end of their lifetimes). At the time Mendeleyev constructed his table, scientists considered atoms to be hard, indivisible spheres. Not until the early 20th century did people realize that the element numbers, beginning with "1" for hydrogen, correspond to the number of particles called protons in the atom.

Mendeleyev's periodic table was an important advance, eventually giving numerous clues about the features and properties of atoms. A modern version of the periodic table of the elements appears as an appendix in this book. Although most of this chapter discusses situations that are not directly linked to the periodic table of the elements, Mendeleyev's work was a critical early voyage into the atomic and molecular realm.

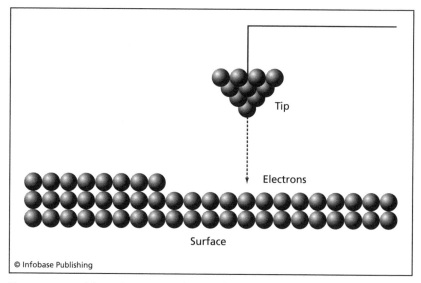

Electrons tunnel from the atom at the tip of the STM probe into the atoms of the surface. The current depends on distance, and as the probe moves it generates an atomic scale map of the material.

occurs. Yet the electrons jump, an unusual phenomenon that is called tunneling. It is explained by a branch of physics, quantum mechanics, which describes the behavior of very small particles such as electrons. According to quantum mechanics, electrons do not have a well-defined position and can tunnel through the small gaps. This is what happens in the STM as the probe slides along just above the material, eventually scanning the whole surface.

The amount of tunneling current is sensitive to the distance between the probe tip and surface. In principle, the STM could measure this distance by measuring the current variation as it scans, but in practice what it does is move the tip up or down to keep the gap—and the current—constant. The amount that the tip moves up or down is measured—this turns out to be easier—and the surface is scanned and mapped, revealing surface features down to the atomic level. The machine is so sensitive that individual atoms can be distinguished.

Surfaces are critically important locations. It is the surface of a solid material that makes contact and interacts with gases, liquids, or other solids, so this is where a lot of action takes place. The STM allows physicists to study surfaces and understand how they form and what happens during reactions with other substances. This knowledge is especially critical to the electronics industry, which builds amazingly small circuits and microchips to fit into compact devices such as laptop computers and cell phones. The first STM appeared in the early 1980s and was so well regarded that two of the developers, Gerd Binnig (1947–) and Heinrich Rohrer (1933–), received a share of the 1986 Nobel Prize in physics.

The STM is not limited simply to reporting the locations of atoms. If the probe gets close enough to the surface, an atom on the surface sometimes adheres to the atom at the tip of the probe. When this happens the surface atom follows the probe as it glides across the material. When the probe tip is retracted, the surface atom falls off. Atoms can be dragged to the desired location and then released, permitting precise atomic construction. Since most objects are made of many millions of atoms, building something atom-by-atom is not generally feasible, but it is possible to construct extremely small objects in this fashion, and this has been done. Electronics, for example, may soon become so miniaturized that it will become necessary to build circuits one atom at a time. In addition, a lot of the atomic designs made with the STM so far have been admired as works of art—which of course can only be "viewed" with the help of the STM itself.

Scientists at the National Institute of Standards and Technology (NIST) reproduced their acronym with cobalt atoms on a surface of copper. The structure is 0.0000016 inches (0.000004 cm) across. *(Joseph Stroscio; Robert Celotta/NIST)*

Beams of Particles

One of the first ways that atoms and their components affected society continues to be the most important. Single particles have little impact due to their small size, but a stream of moving particles—a particle beam—can have a large impact. Beams were important in

Parts of the Atom

Electrons were the first atomic components to be discovered. In 1897, British physicist Sir Joseph John Thomson (1856–1940) was working with vacuum tubes and discovered that beams of particles he called "corpuscles" were being emitted. A vacuum tube is an enclosure of glass in which all or most of the air has been evacuated. The vacuum was necessary because these particles were so small and lightweight that air scattered them and dispersed the beam. Soon the negatively charged particles were named electrons. Thomson received the Nobel Prize in physics in 1906 for his work with electrons and electricity.

The existence of electrons showed that atoms are composed of even smaller components. For a while physicists imagined that atoms were made of a cloud of positive charge with the tiny electrons embedded within it. This picture was proved wrong by New Zealand/British physicist Ernest Rutherford (1871–1937). Rutherford performed an experiment in 1911 in which he fired a beam of positively charged particles called *alpha particles* at a thin sheet of gold; the gold sheet was only a few atoms in width. Expecting that some of the particles would be slightly deflected by the atomic charges, Rutherford and his assistants were shocked to observe that sometimes a particle of the beam reflected backward! Rutherford reasoned that only a compact, positively charged object would be able to reverse the flight of an alpha particle. This was the discovery of the nucleus, the positively charged core of an atom.

A few years later Rutherford identified the positive charges in the nucleus. Using alpha particles as bullets, he fired a beam at various elements such as fluorine, sodium, and aluminum, and knocked out particles that appeared to be the nuclei of hydrogen. These are protons—hydrogen's nucleus normally consists of a single proton. Rutherford based the name *proton* on the Greek word *protos,* meaning first, as in first importance. (The

the discovery of the components of atoms and remain important in physics research as well as in numerous technologies.

Atoms consist of three different particles. At the center of the atom is the nucleus, containing positively charged protons and electrically neutral *neutrons*. The small, compact nucleus is surrounded by a swarm of negatively charged electrons. Atoms

same Greek term is the basis of the name *protein*, which refers to important biological molecules.)

Neutrons were not discovered until British physicist Sir James Chadwick (1891–1974) found them in 1932. Atomic nuclei seemed to be heavier than their proton components would suggest, and scientists had suggested the existence of another particle in the nucleus. The problem was that this particle is not electrically charged and would therefore be difficult to detect, since physicists usually steered and manipulated particle beams with electromagnetic forces. Chadwick did a series of experiments that produced a "radiation" he was able to identify as neutral particles with a *mass* slightly greater than the proton. The term *neutron* conveys the electrical neutrality of the particle. Chadwick received the Nobel Prize in physics in 1935 for this discovery.

As the modern picture of an atom emerged, a peculiar question arose. An atom's nucleus consists of densely packed neutrons and protons, which is not necessarily surprising for electrically neutral neutrons but is quite surprising for positively charged protons. Charges with the same sign repel strongly, so how come the protons can stay packed tightly together? Scientists such as Japanese physicist Hideki Yukawa (1907–81) and others realized there must be a "nuclear" force, called the *strong force*. The strong nuclear force acts only over extremely small distances. Unless protons are close together, the electrical force alone acts upon them and they repel each other. But when protons are pushed together, the strong force becomes a major factor, powerful enough to overcome electrical repulsion.

Physicists have determined the mass of each atomic component with a high degree of accuracy. Protons are about 1,836 times more massive than electrons, and neutrons are 1,840 times more massive. But the nucleus is so tightly packed that an atom, consisting of electrons swarming around the nucleus, is mostly empty space. For instance, the radius of a hydrogen atom is about 100,000 times the radius of its nucleus.

normally have the same number of electrons as protons, and since each of these particles has exactly the same magnitude of charge, the negatively charged electrons offset the positive charge of the protons. A normal atom is therefore electrically neutral. The sidebar "Parts of the Atom" discusses atomic components in more detail.

Electron beams were among the first particle beams that physicists studied, and electron beams have a tremendous number of different applications in today's world, ranging from welding to the manufacturing of minuscule electrical circuits. But perhaps the most common item to use electron beams is called a CRT, which stands for cathode-ray tube. A CRT is at the heart of almost all the older television sets and computer monitors, as well as a large portion of modern video display equipment.

In a CRT, electrons are emitted by a hot surface called a cathode near the narrow end of the tube. A cathode emits electrons when heated. The physicists who first studied this phenomenon did not know that the emission consists of electrons, so they called it a ray and the device became known as a cathode-ray tube. (Sir Joseph John Thomson was the first to realize these rays are electrons, as mentioned in the sidebar "Parts of the Atom.")

High voltages accelerate the electrons emitted by the cathode. A voltage is a difference in electrical potential between two points, creating a force that moves an electrical charge between those points. Electrical charges come in two varieties, positive and negative. Electrons are negative charges and are repelled by other negative charges and attracted to positive charges. A positive voltage—created by a mass of positive charge, for instance—strongly attracts the electrons emitted by a cathode, and in a CRT the electrons accelerate quickly toward the screen and smash into it. The screen is coated with phosphor, which is a substance that emits light when provided energy. The electron collision transfers energy to the phosphor coating, causing it to glow. But exceptionally high voltages—15,000 volts or more—are necessary to produce a high-energy (fast-moving) electron beam; this amount of voltage is 10,000 times that of a typical flashlight battery. These high voltages make CRT televisions and monitors dangerous enough to electrocute careless repair technicians.

Electrons are not only accelerated from the cathode to the screen, they are also concentrated and steered by voltages and magnetic fields along the path. In a black and white television, a single beam scans across the screen dot by dot. The number of electrons in the beam determines the brightness of the dot, and the voltages determine the number of electrons. The signal carrying the picture to be displayed varies these voltages as necessary, so the brightness of each dot is correct and the desired image appears on the screen. The CRT creates a full picture every 30th of a second, and the rapid succession of pictures gives the viewer the perception of continuous motion.

Color televisions have three electron beams and three phosphors that emit red, green, and blue light when struck by its beam. Each dot in a color television is a combination of these three phosphors. The specific amount of red, green, and blue light at each point adds to produce the desired color.

Today many televisions and computer monitors do not have a CRT. Instead they use a liquid crystal display (LCD) or a plasma (these materials will be described later in the book). Compared to CRTs, which are heavy and bulky, LCD and plasma televisions are thin and compact. But CRTs produce an excellent picture at a cheap price, so they will continue to be available for some years to come.

Electron beams are also useful in welding together metals. Conventional welding uses heat to join two pieces of metal to produce a strong, permanent bond. Electron beams create the highest quality welds because the beams can focus a large amount of energy on a small area: The electron is a small particle and a beam of electrons, if tightly concentrated, can be extremely narrow. Electron-beam welding rapidly increased in the late 1950s, and has allowed welders to perform precision jobs that were difficult or impossible with heat torches. Dissimilar metals can be joined, and welds as narrow as a few thousandths of an inch are possible. Electron-beam welding also reduces contamination and distortion, so the weld is more likely to hold.

The United States Postal Service (USPS) uses electron beams for a different purpose. Due to the anthrax contamination of some mail following the terrorist attack on September 11, 2001, the USPS began buying electron-beam systems for irradiation purposes. The energy of electron beams kills any microorganisms that may be stuck to envelopes or parcels, so no contamination of postal equipment or carriers will occur.

Atomic particles other than electrons can make beams and are employed in various industries. Physicians use proton beams, for example, to treat certain types of cancer. Cancer, a disease in which affected tissues grow uncontrollably, is a common illness and the second leading cause of death in the United States. Many treatments for cancer use radiation, either in the form of high-frequency electromagnetic radiation such as X-rays and gamma rays, or in the form of beams of particles such as protons. The goal of the treatment is to kill the affected *cells* while leaving normal, healthy tissue intact. Radiation accomplishes this goal by causing molecules and atoms to become *ions* (electrically charged) by stripping off electrons. This damages the molecule so that it is no longer able to function; if the damaged molecule is an important cellular component such as *deoxyribonucleic acid* (DNA), the cell will usually die.

X-rays and gamma rays are powerful ionizing radiation, but they cannot be as precisely controlled as proton beams. The speed of electromagnetic radiation is not adjustable, but proton velocity can be controlled so that the beam delivers its energy in a more precise spot. This permits physicians to direct the dose of radiation more specifically to the diseased tissue. Bad side effects that often accompany radiation treatment, such as vomiting, are usually caused by unintentional damage to healthy tissue. Proton-beam therapy can reduce the side effects because of its superior precision.

But there are a few problems with proton-beam therapy: It requires expensive equipment, it is effective only for certain types of cancer, and it is not always superior, considering all the factors, to other forms of treatment. Proton beams were used by physicians as early as 1954, but because the required speed and precision are much greater than the electron beams in CRTs, proton accelerators were only available at research institutions. Today the situation has improved and several hospitals and medical centers have made the necessary investment. For example, the Loma Linda University Medical Center in California began a proton treatment center in 1990 and has since treated more than 10,000 patients.

Physicians also use neutron beams to treat cancer patients. Biological tissues interact strongly with neutrons, so the required dosage is much less with a neutron beam than other forms of radiation. Neutrons can be highly effective for treating tumors that are resistant to other treatment options.

But how is a neutron accelerated to the required velocity? While protons and electrons are subject to electrical forces because they are charged particles, neutrons present a problem because they are uncharged. But there are several solutions to this problem. One solution is to attach a proton to the neutron and accelerate the combination to the required velocity, then detach the proton and let the neutron proceed on its own. Another, more common method of producing a neutron beam is to accelerate protons and crash them into the nuclei of atoms. The collision produces a wide array of particles, including neutrons, all carried forward by the impact. Particles other than the neutron are culled out of the beam by bending their trajectory with electric or magnetic fields; what remains are the neutrons. The beam can be narrowed by a series of holed barriers.

Physicists have developed powerful accelerators for all kinds of particles and use these machines to explore the nature of matter. These machines accelerate protons, electrons, and other particles up to nearly the speed of light, which is an astounding 670 million miles/hour (1,072 km/h). In order to accomplish such speeds, the accelerator must be quite large; the accelerator called Large Hadron Collider, being built by CERN (European Center for Nuclear Research) to be completed in 2007, will be one of the largest accelerators ever constructed—17 miles (27 km) in circumference. These particle accelerators are clearly much more expensive and sophisticated than CRTs and hospital-based proton accelerators, but they operate on the same principles. Although costly and requiring huge teams of experts to operate, these machines allow physicists to smash particles together with energies strong enough to tear them apart and create others. By studying the debris, physicists learn more about the fundamental composition of matter.

Nuclear Energy

Particles such as protons can be accelerated to tremendous energies because they are so small and have so little mass. Accelerating a car or a spaceship to anywhere close to the speed of light is impossible today, because the amount of energy required to accelerate an object increases with its mass. But tremendous energies are associated with small collections of particles—the atomic nucleus—for another reason. The basis for this energy, called nuclear energy, also has a lot to do with mass, but in an entirely different way.

German-American theoretical physicist Albert Einstein (1879–1955) made many revolutionary discoveries, but one of his most famous is the equation $E = mc^2$. In the equation, E stands for energy, m for mass, and c is the speed of light in a vacuum. Einstein theorized that objects have a "rest energy" given by this equation; this was a revolutionary idea, since this energy does not depend on motion or any of the familiar mechanical or chemical energies but rather is instead simply based on mass. The equation says that mass and energy are interchangeable, and the exchange rate is quite large. The speed of light is a huge number, equal to 186,200 miles per second (300,000 km/s), and in the equation it is squared, which makes it even larger. Therefore the amount of energy, E, obtained from a mass, m—which Einstein said equals mc^2—is enormous. This equation proved to be correct and set the stage for the development of nuclear energy, both in the beneficial form of nuclear power reactors and in the horrific form of nuclear weapons.

Meanwhile, French physicist Antoine-Henri Becquerel (1852–1908) discovered *radioactivity* in 1896, and Polish scientist Marie Curie (1867–1934) and her husband Pierre Curie (1859–1906) made further advances in this field. Radioactivity is the emission of energy by certain atomic nuclei (plural of nucleus) while they are undergoing transformations, such as a nucleus of the element uranium emitting an alpha particle and turning into a nucleus of the element thorium. (Radioactivity was the source of alpha particles used by Rutherford and others for many of their experiments.) The emissions are spontaneous, occurring without any help or stimulation, at random intervals. All three of these scientists shared the Nobel Prize in physics in 1903 for their work. (Marie Curie also won the 1911 Nobel Prize in chemistry for additional work on radioactive compounds.)

Later, physicists discovered a type of transformation in which an atomic nucleus splits into other, smaller nuclei, a process called *fission*. Fission, like radioactivity, is accompanied by the release of energy but it is generally not spontaneous; uranium, for example, can split into two smaller pieces (nuclei of the elements barium and krypton, for example) but requires the absorption of a neutron. In this process a small amount of mass "disappears": The combined mass of the products—barium, krypton, and several neutrons—is slightly less than the mass of the original uranium nucleus plus the absorbed neutron. This mass becomes energy, in an amount governed by Einstein's equation, $E = mc^2$. Only a small amount of mass (about 0.1 percent) is converted into energy, but the result is gigantic, thanks to the c^2 term in the equation.

These discoveries led to the atomic bomb, developed by scientists working in secret in the United States during World War II. The bombs were made with certain *isotopes* of the elements uranium or plutonium. All atoms of an element contain the same number of protons in the nucleus but some atoms have a variable number of neutrons; the isotopes of an element have the same number of protons but a different number of neutrons. The number of neutrons in the nucleus often affects how much, if any, the nucleus is radioactive, and also affects how easily or not it can undergo fission. The bomb-makers used the isotopes that are most susceptible to fission, of course. These bombs created a chain reaction in which a large number of nuclei simultaneously experienced fission. The chain reaction occurred because a small number of neutrons got the first few nuclei to undergo fission, which produced more neutrons (along with the other products) that could in turn provoke other nuclei to fission—and so on.

Rising 60,000 feet (18,300 m), a column of smoke and dust signals the horrific destruction caused by the atomic bomb dropped on the Japanese city of Nagasaki. *(National Archives and Records Administration)*

To date only two atomic bombs have ever been used in warfare, both dropped by the United States on Japan in World War II. The bombs ended the war, which was what they were intended to accomplish, but the carnage and destruction were terrible. The first atomic bomb was dropped on the city of Hiroshima on August 6, 1945; it had an energy equivalent to 13,000 tons of the high-explosive compound trinitrotoluene (TNT) and killed nearly 100,000 people. The other bomb was dropped on Nagasaki on August 9, 1945, with similar devastation.

Not only are the blasts devastating, but also radioactive materials are scattered as a result. The energy emitted by many of these radioactive isotopes is ionizing radiation and is harmful for the same reasons mentioned earlier—it damages molecules in cells. DNA is particularly vulnerable; damage to DNA can lead to mutations in genes, which may kill a person or animal or cause irreparable, permanent harm. Early physicists who worked with radioactive materials learned of these effects only later, and Marie Curie, for example, died of an illness that was probably caused by the long exposures she endured during the course of her experiments.

The development of nuclear weapons ushered in an era of uneasy peace, as the world's mightiest countries, the United States and the Soviet Union, stocked their armories with vast quantities of bombs. Militaries soon discovered *fusion* devices—the hydrogen or "H-bomb." Fusion, like fission, releases large quantities of energy from atomic transformations, but fusion occurs when small atomic nuclei join together, or fuse to create a larger nucleus. Fusion bombs could be made even more powerful than the fission weapons, and both countries accumulated enough bombs to destroy the world many times over.

This was the era of the cold war, immediately following World War II, between the United States and Soviet Union. The countries had fought on the same side during World War II and emerged as the strongest nations at the end of the war, but political differences turned them into enemies. Both sides detonated many nuclear weapons in tests during the 1950s and 1960s, performed to check the weapon system and as a show of strength. The biggest bomb tested was the Soviet Union's *Tsar Bomba* ("King of the Bombs"), exploded in 1961 over an island in the Arctic Sea. This bomb yielded the equivalent of 50,000,000 tons of TNT, nearly 4,000 times more powerful than the Hiroshima blast. These nuclear weapons were fortunately never used in combat—the war stayed "cold" in the sense that the confrontation involved only threatening words and gestures, not fighting. The cold war ended with the dissolution of the Soviet Union in the early 1990s.

A more productive use of nuclear energy is to convert it into electricity. In the 1950s, soon after the development of the atomic bomb, the first nuclear power plants, or reactors, appeared. These reactors use the same principle as fission bombs but the reactions are controlled—they do not happen all at the same time as in a bomb. All nuclear reactors work by fission; physicists and engineers are working on making fusion reactors, but this type of reaction is much more difficult to control than fission because it requires extreme temperatures. (Fusion is the process by which the Sun and other stars get their energy, and it generally occurs in abundance only under conditions similar to a star's interior, where temperatures reach millions of degrees.) The first large-scale nuclear reactor in the United States, the Shippingport reactor, began operation in Pennsylvania in 1957. According to the International Atomic Energy Agency, nuclear energy provided 16 percent of the total electricity produced in the world in 2002. In the United States, nuclear energy provides about 20 percent of the total amount of electricity.

But beginning around the 1970s, the rate of nuclear reactor construction fell sharply in the United States. Fears of an accidental release of radioactivity swelled public concern. A close call occurred in 1979 at one of the reactors at Three Mile Island near Harrisburg, Pennsylvania, which suffered a partial meltdown, and a small amount of radioactive material escaped. Then, on April 26, 1986, at the Chernobyl nuclear power plant in Ukraine (then part of the Soviet Union), an explosion and fire sent radioactive debris floating across much of eastern and northern Europe. More than 30 people died and hundreds were hospitalized, and hundreds of thousands of people were forced from their homes. The unfortunate consequences of this disaster will continue for years to come, with a probable increase in diseases such as cancer caused by radioactivity exposure.

Opponents of nuclear power point to this disaster as proof that the process is not safe. Not only is there a frightening potential for accidents, but also nuclear reactors produce radioactive waste—the isotopes used as fuel continue to be radioactive long after they are removed from the reactor, so they must be carefully isolated and stored for many years. But as the world's population continues to increase, energy consumption keeps rising and the supply of natural resources such as oil and gas are limited. Another factor to consider is that combustion of oil and gas may contribute to global warming, whereas nuclear power does not. The question of whether nuclear power should play a role in future energy production is an open one. The physics of nuclear power is fairly well understood, but the emotional debate remains.

Molecular Forces

The strong nuclear force is aptly named: Although it only acts over short distances, this force is quite strong. Protons and neutrons are held tightly in the nucleus, to be released only during energetic events such as fission. Other small-scale forces are also important, and, though not quite as strong, they act over longer distances.

Strong chemical bonds form among elements to make compounds. These bonds are not nuclear but arise mainly because of an atom's electrons. In the simplest model of an atom, electrons orbit the nucleus. There are specific properties associated with each orbit; the orbits are grouped in such a way that certain groups, or shells, are most stable when filled. A stable atom is not likely to enter into any chemical reactions. For example, "noble" gases such as helium, neon, and argon are particularly stable and rarely combine to form compounds. Other elements tend to achieve stability by sharing or transferring electrons with atoms of the same element or other elements. The resulting chemical bonds between these elements are strong and long lasting.

Compounds formed by these bonds can have much different properties from the individual elements. One of the most common examples is table salt, sodium chloride, which is a one-to-one combination of the metal sodium and chlorine, a greenish yellow gas at room temperature. Sodium, though metallic, is soft and easily cut with a knife. Chlorine is poisonous; World War I armies occasionally used it as a weapon, and in modern times it is a component in pesticides and mixed into swimming pools to kill germs. The compound formed from these two elements could not be more different. Sodium chloride is a solid *crystal*—it has a regular, repeating structure—and it is essential to life. The bond that holds these elements together is called an *ionic bond:* Sodium donates one of its electrons to chlorine, making both elements stable in terms of their electron energies. This example shows how significantly the properties of materials depend on the arrangement of atomic electrons.

Another type of bond, called a *covalent bond,* arises when atoms share electrons. Covalent bonds are strong, like ionic bonds. But bonds do not always need to be so strong. Sometimes a weaker bond is not only more convenient, but also it is essential. This is the case in one of the most important molecules of all: DNA.

In terms of chemistry, elements combine to form compounds. Physicists often speak of this process as atoms combining to form molecules. Most DNA molecules are gigantic, such as a human chromosome—a long stretch of DNA that contains millions of atoms. (If the DNA of just a single human cell were stretched out, it would be 6 feet [1.83 m] in length!). DNA molecules have a structure known as a double helix, as shown in the figure, and are *polymers*—long chains of molecules bonded together. A DNA molecule is a polymer of molecules called nucleotides, and the structure resembles a long, twisted ladder. The sides of the DNA "ladder" are made from sugar molecules of a type called deoxyribose connected to a phosphate group (phosphorous and oxygen). The rungs (steps) of the ladder are made of four different types of molecules known as nucleobases or, more often, bases: adenine (A), thymine (T), cytosine (C), and guanine (G). The sequence of these bases along the length of the DNA molecule is a language that animal and plant cells read and understand. DNA sequences contain genes that specify a blueprint by which an organism develops and maintains itself.

Heredity is based on DNA and the genes these molecules encode. Genetic information passes from parent to offspring via chromosomes. DNA must therefore be stable—it should not be

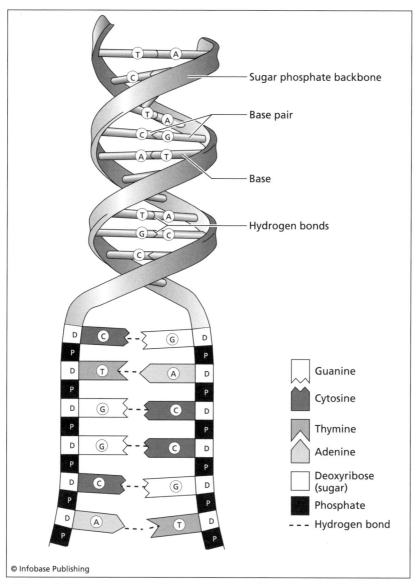

DNA is a double helix with a backbone, composed of phosphate and the sugar deoxyribose, and nucleobases (adenine, thymine, guanine, and cytosine) connected with weak but important bonds. The shape and structure of the nucleobases cause adenine to join only with thymine and guanine to join only with cytosine.

easily broken or damaged; otherwise, the information it contains will become corrupted. As mentioned earlier, ionizing radiation is dangerous because it does just that. But fortunately DNA is otherwise stable, as long as it stays comfortably inside the cell where it belongs.

Although stability is necessary to keep DNA's genetic information intact, that same stability is a problem when the time comes to make use of the information. Before any kind of information is used it must be read in some way or another; a book, for example, can contain the most valuable information in the world yet still be useless if people could not open the cover. A tightly bound book, a manufacturer might argue, is good because it will last a long time—it is stable, in other words. But from the standpoint of readers, such a book is worthless.

DNA deals with this issue by using an important molecular force called *hydrogen bonds*. Hydrogen bonds are weaker than the ionic and covalent bonds mentioned earlier. A hydrogen bond, as the name suggests, is a bond formed partly by hydrogen—a hydrogen atom is one of the bond partners. The hydrogen in a hydrogen bond is already chemically bonded to another atom, such as oxygen and nitrogen. In this chemical bond, the hydrogen atom shares its electron with the other atom, but the sharing is not equal; the other atom is always bigger than tiny hydrogen, the smallest of all atoms, and so its pull on the electron is usually stronger. Because of this, the electron is generally closer to the other atom than hydrogen, which leaves the proton in the hydrogen all alone. The result is a slight positive charge—the hydrogen atom's nucleus is no longer neutralized by its electron. This positive charge attracts atoms that may have a slight negative charge—for instance, the bonded atoms, like oxygen and nitrogen, that tend to pull electrons close to themselves. A hydrogen bond forms by the attraction of the slight or "partial" charges of atoms that have already formed strong chemical bonds.

Hydrogen bonds are important in DNA, as well as in other molecules such as proteins, because they help create the molecule's shape and maintain its stability. In DNA, hydrogen bonds are formed between the bases, as indicated in the figure on page 19. These hydrogen bonds are crucial in holding the double helix together; without them, the two strands would fall apart. But this is just what is needed when the information (the sequence of bases) needs to be read. Because of the relatively weak hydrogen bonds, the DNA double helix is stable but can be easily "unzipped" with the help of other molecules to give cellular processes access to the bases. In this way the genes are transcribed—read out—as necessary. And when the time comes for the cell to divide, the DNA unzips in order to duplicate, so that each of the daughter cells receives its full share. When these processes are complete the hydrogen bonds zip back up the DNA molecule.

Besides DNA, many other substances have properties affected by hydrogen bonds. This includes water, another critical substance in biology, which will be described in chapter 3.

Nanotechnology

DNA and the cellular components that read and duplicate the genetic information are marvelous examples of tiny, molecular machines. Over the years engineers have been designing and building machines on increasingly smaller scales, especially in the field of electronics. A computer microprocessor, for example, can pack hundreds of millions of electronic switches called transistors in a tiny space about the size of a coin. The goal of engineers is to keep miniaturizing technological devices, even going down to the size of atoms and molecules. This is the basis of *nanotechnology*.

In the metric system of measurement the prefix *nano* refers to a billionth, 10^{-9} (the term *nano* is derived from a Greek word meaning midget). A nanometer, for instance, is a billionth of a meter, which equals 0.0000000394 inches. This is the length of a chain of about six carbon atoms. Technology on this scale is certainly a midget; the diameter of an average-sized virus is about 100 nanometers, which is 0.00000394 inches.

Researchers at university laboratories and electronics companies are developing transistors out of small clusters of atoms or molecules, or perhaps only a single molecule. Transistors are important in computer processors because they process large amounts of binary data, as used by computers and many other digital devices. The molecules in "molecular" transistors will be fairly large and usually *organic*—they will contain a backbone of carbon, similar to many of the large molecules such as DNA found in living organisms. Carbon atoms form the backbone of so many large molecules because carbon alone among the common elements readily forms the long chains that such molecules require. (The element silicon is capable of making somewhat long chains, but not as easily as carbon, and these silicon-based molecules are not as stable as carbon-based molecules.)

One promising material for many applications of nanotechnology is called a carbon nanotube. Its structure is similar to a rolled-up sheet of carbon atoms. Carbon nanotubes have surprising strength and can be electrical conductors, meaning that they can carry a current. These properties are surprising since a carbon nanotube resembles a tube of graphite—a soft carbon material that is used in pencils and as a lubricant.

The goal of nanotechnology is not only to fabricate "nanomaterials" with useful properties, but also to construct tiny mechanical or electrical devices—motors, robots, or assemblers. The first section of this chapter mentioned how researchers use STM to build an object atom-by-atom, but this procedure would take too long to make a genuinely useful motor or robot. Instead, researchers tend to be guided by existing "technology"—that is, the molecular machinery that exists inside living cells.

DNA molecules that store information and the molecules that read out and replicate this information are excellent examples of elaborate, tiny biological machinery. Other examples that hold much interest are molecules called kinesin and dynein, which act like motors inside biological cells.

Motors burn fuel and do work. The motor in an automobile converts the energy of a combustible fuel into movement—kinetic energy. Kinesin and dynein, protein molecules found in the cells of many organisms, including humans, are motors that use chemical energy to transport cellular cargo. The interior of cells resembles a city, with thousands of molecules performing critical functions at many different locations. Cargo often needs to be hauled from one place to another. Sometimes the distances can be surprisingly long: A nerve cell in the spinal cord of a person, for example, may need to extend from the base of the spinal cord all the way down to one of the toes. Many operations conducted at the center of the cell generate products that are needed all the way at the end of the cell, which in this case is nearly a yard (0.9 m) away. For nerve cells, the products include neurotransmitters, which are molecules used for communication. If the cell were to rely on diffusion—the random drift of molecules—the required neurotransmitters would rarely arrive at the right spot and the cell would fail to perform its function.

Tiny motor proteins like kinesin and dynein solve this problem. Other molecules in the cell package the needed products into small membrane-bound compartments called vesicles, which then attach themselves to the protein motors. Kinesin and dynein resemble one another and come in several different though similar forms; these molecules are composed of parts or domains attached together. One domain binds to the vesicles so that kinesin and dynein can carry their cargo. Another domain consists of two large, globular ends at the end of two stalks. This is the motor domain, responsible for the movement of the protein. The molecule moves on its "legs"—the two stalks—by binding one of the globular ends to a long filament in the cell, called a microtubule. (Dyneins usually require a little help from other molecules to do this.) Microtubules form part of the skeleton of cells; they are like poles that stretch across the body of the cell and maintain its shape. When one stalk of the kinesin or dynein attaches to a microtubule the other swings forward, binding to the microtubule when it lands. The other stalk then releases its grip and does the same. A protein such as kinesin walks along the microtubule a few nanometer steps at a time until it reaches its destination. It is not all that fast, traveling only about 10 inches (25 cm) a day, but it gets to where it has to go.

All motors need fuel and kinesin and dynein are no exceptions. The required fuel is adenosine triphosphate (ATP). ATP is a molecule produced by an organism's metabolism, which converts glucose obtained from food into ATP. The ATP molecules are a source of chemical energy that supplies many of the operations of the cell requiring energy.

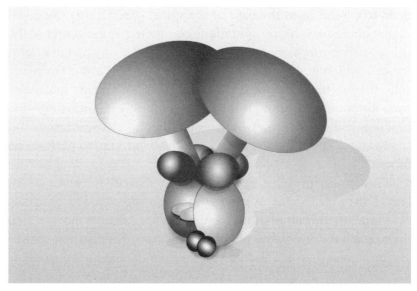

A dynein molecule, illustrated here in simplified form, consists of stalks or "heads" (upper portion of the diagram) to "walk" along thin filaments in the cell called microtubules. *(U.S. Department of Energy Genomics: GTL Program)*

"Nanoengineers" admire kinesin and similar cellular molecules and would like to build devices of the same size and complexity. But kinesins are so effective at what they do that it may not be necessary to start from scratch. Often the best option for engineers is to adapt an existing system to a job. Biologists have been studying kinesin and dynein proteins for several decades, but now engineers have also become interested. The goal is to put together parts of these molecules to build a motor that can perform useful tasks, such as conveying medicines to precise locations in the body.

Other scientists and engineers take a different approach. A team led by Alex Zettl, a physicist at the University of California at Berkeley, built the first nano-scale synthetic (artificial) motor in 2003. The motor consisted of a rotating blade—the rotor—made of gold atoms, attached to a nanotube shaft only a few atoms thick. Electricity powered the device. The whole motor was so small that several hundred would fit in the diameter of a human hair. Because of the motor's incredibly small size, the investigators had to use special microscopes and other sensors to detect its movement.

These small motors may seem like toys or interesting curiosities today, but in the future they may perform many useful tasks. A spinning blade, for instance, might find an application in nano-scale oscillators, switches, mixers, or transportation. But design and engineering at such small scales will not necessarily resemble larger devices simply scaled down; the principles of nanotechnology must be developed on their own. Gravity, for instance, is not a factor in these extremely lightweight devices, and objects that are trivial in the ordinary world—such as a few stray electrical charges—can disrupt the operation of a motor made up of only a few hundred atoms.

Although nanotechnology offers a lot of promise, some people worry about its impact. Engineers would like to build nano-robots that are capable of reproducing. Self-replicating devices could expand their numbers to meet variable demand, but at the same time if the nano-robots got out of control their population could grow to disastrous proportion. Some critics of nanotechnology claim that nano-robots could become like a cancer, which is an unwanted growth of cells in the body. In the worst case scenario these self-replicating devices would spread over the whole world, covering everything with a "gray goo" of nano-robot bodies. This seems unlikely because nano-robots will probably be as sensitive as or more sensitive than living cells, which are also self-replicating but have not caused a global catastrophe. But people must always be aware that both risk and benefits accompany any new technology.

Fantastic Voyages

New technologies such as nanotechnology are frequently the subject of movies. One movie, *Fantastic Voyage,* released in 1966, involved a team of scientists and physicians who were shrunk to microscopic size along with a submarine and injected into an injured human body. Their mission was to maneuver the submarine through the tissues of the patient in order to locate and repair the injury. Along the way they suffered setbacks and had to fight off attacks by the body's immune system, which was intent on destroying what it regarded as invaders. (The movie's plot also formed the basis of a novel, written by science fiction author Isaac Asimov. Asimov published another novel in 1987 on the same subject, titled *Fantastic Voyage II: Destination Brain.*)

Miniaturization to this scale will probably never become possible, but other fantastic voyages are likely in the future. One important goal of nanotechnology, as mentioned earlier, is to build tiny motors or transportation systems to roam the body and deliver medicine or other treatment to diseased tissues. These devices would be a great improvement on existing methods because they are more precise. Medicine from an injection or a swallowed pill travels throughout the whole body, including places that it is not needed, because the physician usually has little control over where the medication goes. Side effects—unintended activity of a medicine—are often caused when the treatment acts on healthy organs or tissues for which it is not meant. A precise delivery system would reduce such occurrences and have the added benefit of concentrating the dose at the right location.

Researchers at Carnegie Mellon University, in Pennsylvania, have recently designed a tiny robot to swim through tissues and *fluids* of the body. Propulsion of the robot cannot be identical to the way that boats or people move through the water; as mentioned previously, conditions on a nanoscale are not the same as in the ordinary world and mechanisms which work on large, everyday scales do not usually apply to the small scale. Instead, the researchers, Bahareh Bekham and Metin Sitti, took their inspiration from common bacteria such as *Escherichia coli*. These tiny bacteria move by waving a whiplike appendage called a flagellum. *E. coli* has no problem maneuvering in the human body, and the researchers hope their robot, once built, will be able to do so as well.

Detection of a disease is as important as delivering medication. Harold Craighead, a physicist at Cornell University in New York, and a team of other scientists have developed a device sensitive enough to detect the presence of only a few virus particles. Consisting of silicon paddles of about 0.000394 inches (0.001 cm) in length and 0.000006 inches (0.000015 cm) wide, the device used the vibration of a crystal to move the paddles back and forth at a frequency of millions of times per second. Attached to the paddles were molecules called antibodies that bind to specific viruses. If a virus bumps into a paddle and gets stuck there, the extra mass, tiny though it is, affects the paddle's motion. Vibration depends on mass, so the extra mass of the virus changes the frequency. Sensitive instruments note the change and report the presence of the virus. Such a device, if used in the body, would be able to identify infectious agents at extremely low concentrations. Treatment could begin so early that the disease would not have a chance to get started.

Medical treatment on a molecular scale is a great future application of atomic and molecular physics, adding to an already impressive list of electron, proton, and neutron beams being used in medicine today. Over the last century technology has progressed rapidly, and an important part of the progress has been a steadily decreasing size—everything is getting smaller. Deriving energy from the nucleus, and detecting and manipulating atoms, such as with the STM, has been achieved. How far nanotechnology will go remains to be seen, but it seems certain that "downsizing" will continue well into the future.

2

STATES OF MATTER

SOLIDS, LIQUIDS, AND gases have different properties: People walk over land, float in water, and move through air. There are three basic states, or *phases,* of matter—solid, liquid, and gas—although many scientists consider plasma (ionized gas) distinct enough to be called the fourth state of matter. All these states will be discussed in this chapter.

The confusion over whether to call plasma a separate state shows that the phases of matter are not always simple and easy to define. Sometimes the properties are deceptive. Water is soft and concrete is not, making a choice between falling in a swimming pool and falling on a sidewalk an easy decision for people to make. Yet water is heavy and massive, so it cannot move quickly. This is not a problem for a diver who hits the water at a slow speed—the water is able to move out of the way—but it is a problem for someone who jumps from a tall height. Hundreds of people have committed suicide by leaping from San Francisco's Golden Gate Bridge into the bay, even though the walkway is only about 220 feet (67 m) above the sea. The water does not cushion the fall because the person's speed is so great that the water cannot get out of the way. Under these circumstances, there is little difference between landing on water and landing on concrete.

Matter is made of tiny particles—atoms and molecules—and the physics of these particle interactions governs the phase of any substance. This chapter shows how the molecules in different phases manage to propel a spaceship, keep an automobile's engine from burning up, and solidify into beautiful works of art.

Matter: Collections of Atoms

The atoms and molecules discussed in the previous chapter assemble themselves into pieces of matter, the phase of which depends on how strongly the particles interact with each other.

At one extreme, the particles practically ignore one another. This is what happens in a gas: The atoms or molecules wander around their container, and although particles bump into each other as well as the container wall, they do not usually stick together and the interaction between them is weak.

The other extreme occurs when all the atoms and molecules stick together. They may be chemically bonded, as in sodium chloride—a compound of sodium and chlorine that is a solid at room temperature—but may also simply be pushed together, as are iron and carbon atoms in steel. Between these two extremes are liquids, where the constituents wander around their container but cohere together as a group.

The state of a substance depends on three factors: temperature, *pressure,* and the nature of the substance itself. All three combine to influence the strength of atomic interactions.

An object at a high temperature feels hot to a person touching it, but on the atomic level temperature is a measure of how fast the object's atoms and molecules are moving. High temperatures mean faster motion; in a hot gas most of the particles are zooming about at tremendous speeds, and in a hot solid they are vibrating rapidly around some central position.

Pressure is a force acting over an area. The molecules of air in the atmosphere exert a force on an object by continually striking it as they fly around in random directions. Scientists quantify this as one atmosphere of pressure; a pressure twice as strong would be two atmospheres, and a pressure only a quarter as strong would be 0.25 atmospheres. At high pressures the molecular collisions become stronger, both to the objects exposed to the air as well as to each other.

Phase Transitions

Oxygen is element number eight and the third most common element in the universe (after hydrogen and helium). Oxygen is vital for life because of its role in turning food into energy (by "burning" glucose), and under dry conditions it composes nearly 21 percent of the Earth's atmosphere. In the atmosphere oxygen is a gas, mostly as two atoms chemically bonded to form an oxygen molecule (O_2), but also as ozone (O_3), especially in the upper atmosphere.

As a gas, oxygen molecules fly around and mix with the other molecules of air (mostly nitrogen, N_2). Oxygen is only slightly soluble in water—only about 0.005 percent of water's weight is oxygen—but this is enough to sustain marine life. But if the temperature is low enough (or the pressure is high enough), oxygen also exists as a liquid. At –297.4°F (–183°C) under normal atmospheric pressure, gaseous oxygen makes a phase transition and changes into a pale blue liquid—liquid oxygen, sometimes called LOX. A person could not breathe it even if the fluid filled the lungs, because such unforgiving cold would freeze the tissue. If the temperature falls even farther, to –361.1°F (–218.3°C), another phase transition occurs: Liquid oxygen freezes and turns solid.

Almost 300 degrees below zero is a frigid temperature, and the molecules move sluggishly. Weak attractive forces exist between molecules, usually due to the arrangement of elec-

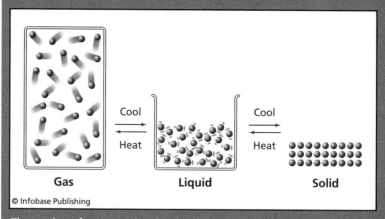

Gas   Cool / Heat   Liquid   Cool / Heat   Solid

© Infobase Publishing

The motion of atoms and molecules decreases and their interactions increase when substances transition from gases to liquids and from liquids to solids.

trical charges; London forces, for example, are due to the attraction of a positively charged nucleus to the electrons of atoms in neighboring molecules. These attractive forces between molecules are much weaker than the chemical bonds between atoms, but when motion decreases and the distance between molecules diminishes, these weak forces become important. As a result, the molecules stick together. The nature and strength of the attractive forces are different for every substance, so the transition temperatures vary. Nitrogen, for instance, goes from a gas to a liquid at $-320°F$ $(-196°C)$.

Liquid and solid oxygen takes up little space compared to the gaseous phase. Since the molecules stick together instead of flying around, LOX is more than 800 times smaller in volume than the gas under the same pressure. But add a little heat and the molecules start moving around with enough energy to break the weakly attractive forces holding the liquid or the solid together. Liquids vaporize and solids melt when the temperature rises. The figure on page 30 illustrates the motion on the atomic and molecular level.

Although increasing temperatures cause phase transitions, the temperature at a phase transition is constant. While oxygen is making a transition between liquid and gaseous phases, the temperature remains at $-297.4°F$ $(-183°C)$. Applying heat to liquid oxygen raises the temperature until $-297.4°F$ $(-183°C)$, the boiling point, is reached; during the process of boiling, the heat does not raise the temperature because the energy goes into breaking the loose bonds that hold the liquid together, instead of making the molecules move faster. The energy of these bonds is sometimes called latent heat. When all the liquid turns to gas, heat will once again raise the temperature. Condensation, the reverse process, also occurs at the same, constant temperature.

Pressure can also cause a phase transition. Oxygen can be a liquid at room temperature if the pressure is high enough—many times stronger than the atmosphere—because the weak attractive forces make the squeezed molecules stick together. Even higher pressures produce solids.

All materials undergo phase transitions. The substance consisting of two atoms of hydrogen and one of oxygen, H_2O, exists as steam, water, and ice, and is important enough to merit its own chapter in this book.

Temperature and pressure influence the phase of a substance because they influence the atomic and molecular interactions. High temperatures mean more motion and more energy for the atoms, giving them a tendency to break any bonds that might otherwise form. High pressure, on the other hand, pushes the atoms together and provides more opportunity for interactions. The nature of the substance is also an important factor, because all materials exhibit a certain phase at specific temperatures and pressures. The sidebar discusses phase transitions, the points at which a substance melts (a transition from the solid phase to a liquid) and evaporates (liquid to gas transition).

As a gas, oxygen has plenty of industrial uses—it is a reactive substance that forms a part of many compounds as well as supporting life—and businesses that use oxygen often need to store and transport it. But the stored and transported oxygen is usually a liquid, not a gas; a gas takes up a huge amount of space, while the same amount of material, as a liquid, is hundreds of times smaller. As explained in the sidebar, oxygen is a liquid only when extremely cold or under a tremendous amount of pressure. Despite the expense of maintaining these conditions, hauling a tank of liquid oxygen is cheaper than transporting a mountainous container of gas. The reduced volume is particularly important in launching a rocket or ship into space, even though the propellant will be in the gas phase.

Gases: Making Rockets Go

Rockets operating in the airless void of space must carry not only fuel but also the oxygen needed for the fuel to burn. Trying to lift the weight of a bulky container of gas would be far too expensive, so liquid oxygen offers a much cheaper alternative. A space shuttle's external tank contains a combination of liquid hydrogen and liquid oxygen that burns at a temperature of about 4,530°F (2,500°C).

But as explained below, a gas is what rockets need the most—gas is the propellant that makes a rocket go. Rockets do not have pistons or turbines like the internal combustion engines of cars or airplanes, since there is no ground for wheels to push against or air to provide a lifting force for wings. Propulsion in the vacuum of space uses Newton's third law of motion: For every action there is an equal and opposite reaction.

Newton's third law also holds here on Earth. When a rifle fires a bullet, the projectile flies away at a great speed, but the rifle also moves in the other direction, though not as much. The rifle has a much greater mass than the bullet, particularly if it is held snugly by the shooter; with all that mass, the reaction—the "kick" of the rifle—is equal to the action (the flying projectile) but the speed is a lot less. All processes conserve momentum, which is the product of an object's mass, m, and velocity, v, and a large-mass rifle and shooter with a small velocity offsets a small-mass projectile sent flying away in the opposite direction at a high velocity.

In space, rocket engines expel mass out the back end of the craft, providing a forward thrust by Newton's third law. For example, a space shuttle has three main rocket engines, each of which uses the liquid hydrogen–liquid oxygen combination for fuel. Combustion generates hot, expanding gases that are funneled out of a nozzle at a velocity of roughly 10,000 miles per hour (16,000 km/h). The three engines have a maximum capability of 37 million horsepower, as powerful as 100,000 of the fastest cars on the road.

Even though they are enormous, the three main engines of a space shuttle are not the primary means of thrust during liftoff. These engines provide some of the power needed for launching, but their main job comes later, when the pilot maneuvers the ship into orbit. Two-thirds of thrust at liftoff comes from two 149-foot (45.5-m) solid rocket boosters (SRBs) strapped to the ship. As the name suggests, the SRBs get their propellant from burning solid fuel—each rocket has more than a million pounds of fuel, consisting of a mixture of an ammonium perchlorate, aluminum, and binding agents. The SRBs expend their fuel and drop off when a space shuttle reaches an altitude about 150,000 feet (45.7 km); the reusable rockets descend with parachutes and make a soft landing in the ocean, where vessels are waiting to recover them.

The space shuttle *Endeavour* lifts off on June 5, 2002. One of the two solid rocket boosters can be seen attached to the side of the external fuel tank, which is the large cylindrical object located underneath the shuttle. *(NASA)*

Liquids: Keeping the Wheels Turning

Rockets burn liquid or solid fuel to generate the hot gases needed for propulsion. Propelling a rocket by forcing liquids or solids out of the nozzle would also work but would not be very efficient—the force would have to come from some kind of explosion, like an explosion of gunpowder that sends a bullet at high speed out of a rifle barrel. Instead of carrying along extra mass, a rocket uses the products of the explosion itself—expanding gases—as propellant.

But liquids can do jobs that gases cannot. Not only does the burning of a liquid fuel called gasoline provide the power for most automobiles, but also liquids are vital in keeping the wheels turning for another reason. The enemy to conquer here is friction.

Many automobile engines have four, six, or eight pistons whose back-and-forth motion turns the crankshaft, which in turn rotates the axles and wheels. A cylinder encloses each piston, and expanding gases of combustion drive the piston's motion. The piston must fit snugly inside the cylinder, otherwise the gases would rush around the piston instead of pushing against it. But this means the piston rubs against the walls of the cylinder. Two objects that rub against each other generate heat because of friction; even when the surfaces are smooth, friction between moving parts robs the process of a considerable quantity of energy and wastes it as unwanted heat.

There is a lot of friction in automobile engines because there are a lot of moving parts. Heat increases with the speed of the motion, as does the wear and damage of the parts. The components of an engine must fit tightly but it is essential to minimize the extent to which they rub against each other. This is a job for lubrication—and an excellent lubricator is oil.

To minimize friction, oil must be the right thickness, as measured by its *viscosity*. A low-viscosity liquid is thin and runny, and a high-viscosity liquid is thick and syrupy. If the viscosity is too low the oil fails to coat the moving parts, so it does not alleviate friction. If the viscosity is too high the engine parts have to move through a sludge that slows them down or sometimes even stops them altogether.

Maintaining the proper oil viscosity is a problem because of temperature effects. High temperatures mean that a substance's atomic and molecular components jitter around much more, a condition that tends to thin out a liquid. Low temperatures thicken liquids. But cars must operate in all kinds of temperatures: An engine that has been running for a while gets hot, but when first started the engine is cold—particularly on a cold January morning in Duluth, Minnesota, where the thermometer might register zero degrees.

Oil manufacturers solve this problem by adding specific molecules to the mixture. One common additive is called poly(lauryl methacrylate), consisting of a long chain of molecules—a polymer. When the temperature is high, the chain jitters around and stretches out to its full length; the oil molecules bump against it, hindering their motion. As a result, the oil does not lose its viscosity when it gets hot. At low temperatures the chain curls up and stays

Oil and other components of race car engines must be able to withstand the rigors of extreme heat and motion. *(United States Army/Major William Thurmond)*

out of the way, so the polymers do not increase the viscosity when the oil is cold.

Manufacturers rate engine oil with two numbers, such as 5W30 or 10W30. The first number describes the oil's viscosity in low-temperature (winter) conditions, and the second in high-temperature conditions. These numbers do not have units, they are relative—they only have meaning when compared to each other—and the lower the number, the lower the viscosity. An oil rated at 5W30 functions better during extreme winters than 10W30. Race cars operate under extreme conditions all the time, reaching speeds of more than 220 miles per hour (352 km/h) and rotating up to 19,000 revolutions per minute (a rotation rate that would tear apart an ordinary automobile engine). In many cases these oils are synthesized from special materials and perform under conditions in which the oil temperature exceeds 250°F (121°C) and can even reach 300°F (149°C). Because of these temperatures, the upper range of racing oil viscosity needs to be 50 or 60.

Solids: Making Statues

Solids, like liquids and gases, are also important in ships and transportation. Certain fuels are solid—such as some kinds of rocket fuel, before it is burned—and the frame of the vehicle must be made from a sturdy material. Solids can have different forms, some of which are composed of geometrically precise units and some of which have little, if any, internal structure.

The sturdiness and fixed shape of solids has also long been used to create expressive, lasting symbols—art. Art flourished in ancient cultures such as Greece, and creative people learned how to shape metals like bronze into beautiful statues. Metal is a splendid material—shiny and strong—but shaping it can be a troublesome task. One of the best methods to do this involves phase transitions at crucial steps in the process.

The lost-wax process of casting bronze begins with a wax model. In the simplest version of this technique, the artist carefully sculpts the soft wax into the figure that he or she wants to create, then covers the wax model with a layer of clay. The clay conforms to the shape of the wax and, when heated, hardens into a mold. During the heating process the wax melts and is poured out of the clay mold (this is the "lost wax" part of the process). Casting is next. Bronze is a metal *alloy* of about 90 to 95 percent copper and 5 to 10 percent tin, and melts at temperatures around 1,830°F (1,000°C), depending on the composition. Heated and molten bronze fills the mold. When the metal cools and solidifies, the artist breaks the mold and polishes the statue.

A disadvantage of this method is that the artist loses the wax model, which can take a lot of time and effort to make—the model, after all, is what the end product will look like, so it must be perfect. If something goes wrong with the bronze casting, the artist has to start all over again. This is why many artists prefer a technique known as the indirect method of lost-wax casting, in which the model is not destroyed. In this technique the model, usually made of clay, provides the form that is replicated by a

This statue of a Viking explorer, Thorfinn Karlsefni, is at Fairmount Park in Philadelphia, Pennsylvania. *(Kyle Kirkland)*

mold made of wet pieces of plaster or clay. After peeling off the dried pieces, the artist assembles them into a mold and lines it with a thin layer of wax. When the wax cools and hardens, the mold is removed and the artist carefully checks and corrects the shape. Then another mold is made, and from there the process is similar to the direct method of lost-wax casting. But the original clay model remains.

The lost-wax method became popular in Greece as this culture blossomed in the fifth century B.C.E. Much of this art did not survive to the present today, because the valuable metal was later melted down and reused for other, less creative projects. Most of the splendid Greek statues housed at museums such as the Metropolitan Museum of Art in New York City are marble copies, sculpted by artists in the Roman era. The original bronze statues are gone for good.

Sometimes this process goes in the reverse direction, to the delight of admirers of art and peace. The statue of Andrew Jackson at Lafayette Square in Washington, D.C., near the White House, is made out of bronze obtained from melting the cannons captured by Jackson's troops in the War of 1812.

Plasmas for Propulsion, Television, and Fusion

A change in bronze—going from a cannon to a molten phase and then being cast back into a solid state as a statue of a U.S. president—took a lot of effort and artistry. A change in state of a gas into a plasma does not require as much work: Stripping an electron away from gaseous atoms, such as by applying extreme heat, electric fields, or high-energy radiation, produces ions. Ionized gas is called a plasma.

Plasmas are the most common state of matter in the universe, although they did not receive a lot of attention until the middle of the 20th century. Stars such as the Sun are gigantic spheres of gas that is hot enough to be ionized—a plasma. Plasmas also appear on Earth, during lightning and in a certain layer of the atmosphere called the ionosphere. The importance of plasmas in science and technology today arises from their electrical properties; consisting of charged particles, ionized gases are by their nature electrical. Even gases in which only a few percent of the atoms or molecules are ionized can behave more like plasmas than an ordinary, electrically neutral gas.

As discussed in the previous sections, modern rockets burn a liquid or solid fuel to create a hot, expanding gas that propels the craft by Newton's third law, throwing atoms and molecules out the rear nozzle to generate forward thrust. But in the future, the combustion of a fuel to produce a fast-moving gas may be unnecessary. Accelerating plasma ions by electromagnetic fields may prove to be easier, cheaper, and more efficient.

The idea behind plasma propulsion is simple: Create a plasma by ionizing a gas and apply electric and magnetic fields to push the ions out of the rear nozzle. The effect is the same as directing the products of combustion out the nozzle, since expelling mass—ions in this case—achieves thrust. One big advantage is that burning a fuel is not necessary, so rockets could be free from the burden of carrying fuel as well as oxygen or an oxygen compound to support combustion. Carrying a propellant would still be necessary—and for the sake of reduced volume the propellant would be stored as a liquid or solid, as it is in today's spaceships—but that is all. After a phase transition to a plasma, the propellant is ready go. The reduced weight would make space launches much easier, since less mass requires less force to lift.

NASA already has projects under way to test and develop ships using plasma propulsion. One project, initiated in 2005, involves scientists and engineers at the University of Texas at Austin, the University of Alabama at Huntsville, and NASA's Marshall Space Flight Center in Huntsville and the Johnson Space Center in Houston, Texas. The innovative goals are to design nozzles that can guide and direct the exit of plasma, and finding the most efficient technique to generate thrust from this type of propulsion. Strong electromagnetic fields can eject plasmas at tremendous velocities, so this method of propulsion, if properly developed, will produce a huge amount of thrust. NASA expects this new class of ships to play a role in the future exploration of Mars and the rest of the planets in the solar system.

Plasmas can also give off useful amounts of radiation. The bright neon signs that light up cities during the nighttime are made from excited plasmas—in a tube with a strong electric field, neon ions emit electromagnetic radiation. Plasma discharges make good televisions in a similar way; the screen consists of hundreds of thousands of small cells containing ionized neon or xenon gas that emit ultraviolet radiation when excited. Although this radiation is invisible, phosphor coatings absorb it and emit light. Plasma televisions are bright, have excellent contrast, and can be made with wide, thin screens. They are also quite expensive, although prices will drop as manufacturers develop cheaper designs and materials.

There is another, potentially crucial use of plasmas in technology. As in the heart of the Sun and other stars, physicists would like to use plasmas to generate power from fusion. Fusion is a reaction in which small atomic nuclei join to make a larger nucleus, and in the process, a vast amount of energy is liberated. Bombs have been made from rapid fusion reactions, but to produce steady, useful amounts of energy to light and heat homes and businesses, controlled fusion is necessary. Fusion occurs in the plasma of the Sun because of the enormous temperatures— about 27,000,000°F (15,000,000°C) in the core—and duplicating these conditions on Earth is not easy. But if successful, fusion offers the world a much needed cheap and plentiful supply of energy.

The promise of plasmas is great. Like all phases of matter, ionized gases have specific properties, although these properties are often similar to those of other states. Plasmas "flow" in response to electromagnetic forces, like oil flowing in the crevices of an engine to protect the moving parts. Although plasmas are not solid and sturdy like the bronze of a statue or the steel of a tank or rocket, their ionized particles participate in strong electrical interactions that produce sturdy forces for propulsion and lighting. And of course plasmas are most like gases, since they fly around and fill the volume of their container. But even if some people do not consider plasmas a distinct state of matter, they will probably make a huge difference in the future of technology.

3
WATER

THE WATER FLOWING from a tap or a showerhead looks fresh, clean, and new. Utility companies spend a lot of time and money to filter out impurities, so freshness and cleanliness should be expected. But tap water is hardly new—most of it is as old as Earth. At one time, long ago, a dinosaur may have set its foot in the same water that now fills a glass, waiting to be sipped.

Most people go ahead and drink the water anyway, perhaps relying on the water company to remove all traces that any dinosaur may have left—or perhaps not realizing how old, and strange,

Niagara Falls, on the Niagara River, straddles the border between New York and the Canadian province of Ontario. This view is from the Canadian side. About 100,000 cubic feet (2,800 m³) of water falls each second during a summer day (the flow rate varies, governed by the hydroelectric plants along the river). *(Elizabeth Kirkland)*

water can be. Water is one of the lightest molecules in the world and is a compound of two of its most reactive elements—two atoms of hydrogen and one atom of oxygen, symbolized chemically as H_2O. This is an amazing compound, unique in a lot of ways: It exists in all three states—solid, liquid, and gas—on Earth's surface, it expands when frozen, and it dissolves almost anything. This chapter describes these astonishing properties and reveals why people must drink water, even if it once squished between the clawed toes of *Tyrannosaurus rex*. To all life on Earth, water is essential.

Life's Most Important Molecule

The human body is nearly 70 percent water by weight; for a person weighing 150 pounds, more than 100 pounds is water. Water fills the trillions of cells that compose the organs and tissues of the body, and it makes up a substantial portion of the fluid that surrounds the cells. Blood also contains a lot of water, which is why it flows so easily through veins and arteries.

Water molecules are stable but a small number dissociate—they split into two parts, a hydrogen ion (H^+) and a hydroxide ion (OH^-). Chemists write this reaction as

$$H_2O \longleftrightarrow H^+ + OH^-.$$

The double-headed arrow means the reaction proceeds in both directions. Acids such as sulfuric acid, found in automobile batteries, have more hydrogen ions than hydroxide ions, and in bases such as sodium hydroxide, used in making soaps and paper, the opposite situation holds. Pure water is neutral, with the same number of hydrogen and hydroxide ions.

Although only a few H_2O molecules dissociate, all water molecules have a peculiar property that is critical to their role in living organisms. Water is sticky: Its molecules pull on each other and on any other substance they contact. This makes water an excellent solvent, because many substances readily dissolve in H_2O. A large number of these substances are crucial for the many chemical reactions that underlie life. Dissolved in the water inside cells and tissues of the body are a huge number of important molecules; within these cellular solutions occur the reactions that break food down into energy and grow and maintain structures and organs. The reason water is a good solvent has to do with the physics of its molecular structure—H_2O is a polar molecule, as explained in the sidebar.

Even though people sometimes call water the "universal solvent," it does not dissolve everything. If water dissolved everything, a person jumping into a swimming pool would be making a fatal mistake. Polar substances such as salts and acids dissolve in water because the polar molecules of H_2O attract and pull apart the components, but nonpolar substances such as fats and oils stay together. Oil and water do not mix, and since oil is lighter, spills from tanker ships float on the sea. Membranes surrounding biological cells are mostly made of fats called lipids that do not dissolve in water, and connective tissue holding together the cells of human and animal bodies are made of proteins that are also insoluble—so a person who jumps into a swimming pool stays intact.

The substances dissolved in water are critical for life. Nutrients, enzymes, and ions are essential to carry out the chemical reactions of metabolism that maintain and support all living creatures, and water is the substance in which these reactions take place. Animals and people lose water from sweating and respiration (some water escapes from the lungs), and what is lost must be replaced. Maintaining ionic balance is also necessary; in order for the body to work, ions such as sodium, potassium, chloride, calcium, and others must exist at a certain concentration—no more, no less. Drinking salty sea water is a bad idea because the ions accumulate in the body and the concentrations become too high; the brain is particularly vulnerable to ionic imbalances, causing stranded sailors who drink too much sea water to get dizzy and confused.

Other jobs of water in biology include temperature regulation (by sweating) and lubrication (the joints, for instance). Another

Polar Molecules

Hydrogen bonds, discussed in chapter 1, are important in the behavior of water. The oxygen nucleus has a greater pull on the molecule's shared electrons than the tiny nuclei of hydrogen, creating small areas where the electric charges of the molecule do not balance. This creates electric fields, tiny in magnitude but still capable of attracting and influencing other molecules. The molecular structure of H_2O is shown in the figure. The positive and negative fields form a dipole—two poles, or ends, of charge—and such molecules are called polar. Temporary bonds form when molecules approach one another, because the positive and negative charges attract (in electricity, opposite charges attract and like charges repel). The positive hydrogen end of one water molecule and the negative oxygen end of another form a bond called a hydrogen bond. These bonds are about 20 times weaker than the covalent chemical bond holding together the oxygen and hydrogen of a single water molecule, but hydrogen bonds have important effects.

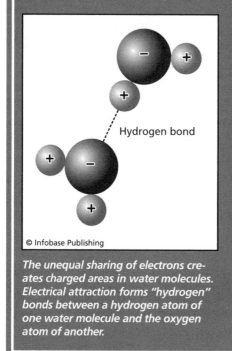

© Infobase Publishing

The unequal sharing of electrons creates charged areas in water molecules. Electrical attraction forms "hydrogen" bonds between a hydrogen atom of one water molecule and the oxygen atom of another.

essential function involves water's ability to defy gravity—at least in a thin tube.

Climbing Up Thin Tubes: Capillary Action

The polar molecules of water latch onto each other as well as any additional polar molecules that happen to be in the vicinity. This

Since water is entirely composed of hydrogen and oxygen, it comes as little surprise that hydrogen bonds form when molecules of H_2O come together. These weak, temporary bonds enable the molecules to stick together more than other compounds that do not form hydrogen bonds, and as a result H_2O is a liquid at higher temperatures than a lot of other substances. Water exists between 32°F (0°C) and 212°F (100°C) at sea level, a much warmer range than a substance such as oxygen, described in chapter 2, with a liquid range of −361.1°F (−218.3°C) to −297.4°F (−183°C). Even hydrogen sulfide, H_2S, with its similar formula and structure, is a gas instead of a liquid at room temperature because it does not form as many hydrogen bonds.

Not only do the polar molecules of water latch onto each other, but also they grab hold of other molecules, particularly those that also have poles or areas of small electrical charges. Thanks to these electrical forces, table salt—sodium chloride—dissolves in water because the polar H_2O molecules wedge apart the bond made when sodium donates an electron to chlorine. The electron stays with chlorine, and so floating around in salt water are a lot of positively charged sodium ions and negatively charged chloride ions. These charges are mobile, which means that salt water, unlike pure water, can carry a hefty electric current.

Polarity is also the reason microwave ovens cook food. The electromagnetic fields of microwave radiation vary at about 2.5 billion times a second, swishing the polar molecules of water back and forth at a tremendous rate. The energetic motion raises the water's temperature and heats anything containing a lot of water, such as most foods, while having little effect on dry materials such as plates or dishes.

stickiness lets water perform another trick—climbing up a narrow opening.

Rather than spreading out in a thin film, water tends to bunch together in droplets. This is because of the interaction between its polar molecules; since they attract one another, the cohesive force keeps them from scattering. Heat can pry them apart, but it takes a high temperature—water boils at a higher temperature than many other substances, even though its molecules are light and mobile. The attraction between these polar molecules creates a force called *surface tension*. Water acts like it is under *tension* because the molecules stick together and are difficult to pull apart.

Water's polar molecules also adhere to surfaces that are lined with polar molecules, such as glass. These forces are similar to the cohesive forces between molecules but can be even stronger. In a glass of water, the water's surface rises slightly at the edges, where it meets the glass—this is called a meniscus. The polar molecules stick to the glass, and, because the adhesion is so strong, they "climb" a small way up the sides. If the glass is extremely narrow, such as a thin tube or capillary, the molecules sticking to the sides lift themselves up until their weight finally stops them. Blood, which is mostly water, squeezes through

Soldiers deployed in the desert may need to supplement their water ration with a solar still. Sunlight passes through a transparent plastic cover and warms the ground, evaporating moisture that rises and condenses on the plastic. *(United States Air Force/Captain Karalyne Lowery)*

about 50,000 miles (80,000 km) of tiny capillaries in the human body.

Capillary action is critical in tall plants such as redwood trees, common in California. In a race for sunlight, redwood trees can grow to a height of about 330 feet (110 m), and drawing up water to nourish the cells at the top is a problem. A vacuum pump will not work beyond about 33 feet (10 m), so another method must suffice—capillary action. The forces between polar molecules are so powerful that they would support a column of water several miles high. Although this would seem to give trees the means to push higher, the capillaries would have to be so thin that not enough water would reach the top. A trade-off between height and volume results in a maximum height of about 330 feet (110 m), so redwood trees cannot grow much taller without running into a water shortage at the summit. This means that Jack and his beanstalk—the one that climbed into the sky, reaching all the way to the giant's home—made a good story but physics does not quite allow it to happen in reality.

How Bugs Walk on Water

Although water will not allow beanstalks to reach orbital altitudes, surface tension is responsible for a clever trick—bugs walking on the surface of a pond.

Water striders (also called pond skaters) are common bugs that are found on ponds and slow-moving streams. And they are actually on, rather than in, the water; although the bug's density is greater than water, it does not sink. Polar molecule cohesion is strong enough to form a "skin" on the surface of a pond or stream, and a small weight, such as a bug or a thin metal needle, does not break through the surface because it does not generate enough pressure to pull apart the bonds.

An adult water strider can reach a size of about half an inch (1.25 cm) and, like all insects, has six legs. The middle pair of the legs is long, and the animal uses them to propel itself forward, pushing gently against the surface of the water. This locomotion is a delicate task, and a small amount of water is necessarily put into motion at the same time; scientists are still uncertain whether the insects generate their forward momentum by creating complex waves or swirls in the water. Researchers David Hu, Brian Chan, and John Bush at the Massachusetts Institute of Technology built a tiny robot similar to a water strider after studying the insects for some time. In a paper published in 2003 in the journal *Nature,* "The Hydrodynamics of Water Strider Locomotion," the scientists suggested that the bugs create vortices—spiraling or whirling liquid—that flow backward underneath the surface of the water, propelling the bug in the opposite direction like a rocket spewing propellant from a rear nozzle.

Snow and Ice

Life in and around the water has much more than just surface tension to appreciate. The phase of H_2O often changes with the season—water in summer, snow and ice in winter—yet lakes and ponds usually do not freeze solid. The surface freezes but the bottom stays liquid, giving plants and animals a chance of survival.

Phase transitions are part of the great cycle of H_2O on the planet. A small number of molecules gets made or destroyed by chemical reactions, but most of the H_2O on Earth cycles between phases: liquid to vapor by evaporation, condensing in the upper atmosphere back to liquid or solid, then precipitation in the form of rain or hail.

Some of the water in ponds, lakes, and oceans stays in place but also goes through phase transitions during the course of a year. In certain climates of the Northern Hemisphere, such as Canada, northern United States, and northern Europe, winters are cold enough to freeze small bodies of water and streams, and even rivers. (This is also true of regions in the Southern Hemisphere, in places such as Tierra del Fuego, at the tip of South America.) But because of the physics of water, these bodies of water do not sim-

Winters are sometimes cold enough to ice the surface of even a large river such as the Susquehanna, shown here at Harrisburg, Pennsylvania. *(Elizabeth Kirkland)*

ply become blocks of ice. Except for shallow ponds and streams, a layer of water remains at the bottom.

Bodies of water seldom freeze solid because H_2O is one of the few substances in the world that expands when it freezes. Cooler temperatures normally cause a material to contract—the molecules move more slowly and do not press out as much, so the volume decreases. But frozen water is different, and ice is less dense and therefore floats in water. The density decreases because hydrogen bonds, mentioned earlier in the chapter, create forces that push and pull the molecules as they settle into a solid form, and the resulting structure has a geometry called hexagonal (a polygon having six sides). The hexagonal shape of ice crystals has a slightly larger volume than the same amount of material in liquid form, so its density is less.

The maximum density of water occurs around 39°F (4°C), slightly above the freezing point (32°F or 0°C). Water cooled to this temperature behaves as any other material does and contracts (though not much), but once this point is reached water begins to expand and continues through the freezing point. Since substances with greater densities tend to sink, water at 39°F (4°C) sinks in water at any other temperature. As the water of a freezing lake reaches 39°F (4°C) it sinks and displaces the colder water, which rises toward the surface and freezes. The bottom, though not balmy, tends to stay above freezing.

Another consequence of floating ice is not so pleasant. Each year about 10,000 to 20,000 blocks of ice calve (separate) from gigantic glaciers in Greenland and the Arctic during the relatively warm spring and summer months. Glaciers form when falling snow accumulates over time and compresses into ice. The huge weight of the ice causes the glacier to flow, like a river of ice, sometimes as fast as 50 feet (15.2 m) or more a day. After several thousand years the ice arrives at the edge of the continent (or ice shelf, if

This "river" of ice is located near the southern tip of South America. *(Elizabeth Kirkland)*

the ice extends over the ocean). Waves and tidal action gradually dislodge pieces of the glacier, calving blocks of ice called icebergs that float away in the sea.

Icebergs come in different shapes and sizes. Icebergs the size of a car are called growlers by the old sailors of the sea, and icebergs as big as a house are called bergy bits. Some icebergs can be enormous, such as the one named B15 that broke away from Antarctica's Ross Ice Shelf in March 2000. This iceberg was as big as the state of Delaware and officially belonged in the descriptive category known as "Very Large."

Most icebergs do not travel far, and perhaps only 1 percent of those calved in Greenland reach the waters of the Atlantic Ocean. But the northern Atlantic Ocean is cold, so any large iceberg that rides the ocean currents into the Atlantic will take time to melt. Adding to their lifespan is their ability to absorb a great deal of heat before they melt; because the polar H_2O molecules hold together so well, it takes a lot of energy to pull them apart. Icebergs are a hazard to shipping, and the most

Air Force airmen stand on a iceberg in the Arctic Ocean. *(United States Air Force)*

famous disaster occurred when the RMS *Titanic* scraped across an iceberg, tearing a hole in its hull and sinking in the Atlantic Ocean. No one knows the size of this iceberg but the survivors estimated it was about 100 feet (30.5 m) high and 300 feet (91.5 m) long. But since ice is only slightly less dense than water, most of an iceberg's mass (about 7/8 of the total) is beneath the surface.

Much less dangerous is snow. This solid form of H_2O falls when water in the upper atmosphere freezes and begins to fall. When the air near the surface is warm, as in spring and summer, the ice melts and reaches the ground as rain. In the colder months, the lower atmosphere is also cold and the pellets of ice grow as they pass through the layers of air. Different temperatures cause the ice crystals of snow to grow in different ways; when close to the freezing point the crystals form plates, but at colder temperatures they are shaped more like columns. At even colder temperatures, near 0°F (–17.8°C), the familiar starlike snowflakes form. As the snowflakes fall through the atmosphere's layers, they encounter varying conditions and temperatures, and since no two flakes experience exactly the same conditions, each crystal grows in its own individual pattern.

The first person to demonstrate that no two snowflakes are alike was a self-educated Vermont farmer, Wilson "Snowflake" Bentley (1865–1931). Bentley collected more than 5,000 snowflakes, publishing photographs of many of them in magazines and journals. All the snowflakes were unique.

Seeding Clouds and Making Rain

Farmers who live in warmer climates than Bentley often wish for water in any form, whether rain, hail, or snow. Droughts caused by below-average rainfall can devastate crops and ruin an entire growing season.

One of the worst droughts experienced in the United States occurred during a particularly trying time. In the 1930s, in the midst of a disastrous economic depression, the Great Plains of the Midwest suffered a severe drought. The Oklahoma panhandle, Texas, Kansas, eastern Colorado, and New Mexico became the "Dust Bowl," where winds blew dry, loose soil in vast dust clouds across the prairies. Combined with the economic hardship of the Depression, the drought forced many thousands of farmers to abandon their farms, hop into battered trucks, and head to California.

Earth has a lot of water, a total of about 325 million cubic miles (1.3 billion km^3) of it, spread out over the whole planet. No one is sure where this water came from originally, but there is a theory that comets brought most of it to Earth as they smashed into the planet over the course of millions of years. A comet is a dirty snowball; with a diameter averaging between 0.6–12 miles (1–20 km), a comet consists of dust, ice, and frozen gases orbiting the Sun. The orbit of most comets takes them deep out into space, but upon their approach to the Sun the comet warms up and some of the ice and gas boil away, forming a tail that can sometimes be seen from Earth. Over a period of time early in Earth's history, a bombardment of comets may have brought some or perhaps most of the planet's water.

The 325 million cubic miles of H_2O on the planet may seem like a lot, but most of it is unavailable for human use. The oceans, icecaps, and glaciers have 99 percent of the total, and freshwater in the ground, lakes, atmosphere, and rivers compose less than 1 percent. Although these percentages remain fairly constant, water is always in motion, going through a cycle of evaporation, condensation, precipitation—in the form of rain, snow, or hail—and collection in lakes and rivers.

The limited amount of fresh, potable (drinkable) water is a precious resource that must be conserved. But the water cycle does not distribute this resource evenly. Areas of the Sahara in Africa may enjoy only one or two rain showers a year, while rain comes almost every day on Mount Waialeale in Kauai, one of the Hawaiian Islands. This unequal distribution makes some people wonder if science and technology can be used to even things out a little bit.

Making rain is not as easy as it sounds. In order for rain to appear, there must already be a sizable quantity of moisture in the atmosphere, since no one can make rain fall from dry air. Clouds are a sign of moisture—high-altitude clouds are mostly made of ice crystals and low-altitude clouds are mostly water droplets—but they do not guarantee rain. Natural rainfall occurs when microscopic particles of dust, salt crystals, or smoke floating in the atmosphere act as condensation nuclei, attracting water or ice. (Condensation nuclei should not be confused with atomic nuclei.) When the water or ice grows heavy it falls as a drop of rain or snow.

Cloud seeding is an attempt to help this process along by providing condensation nuclei. Dry ice, silver iodide, or other particles spilled from a plane or shot upward from the ground offer condensation nuclei on which moisture in the atmosphere can settle. Ever since the first attempt to create artificial clouds in 1946 by Vincent J. Schaefer, working at the General Electric Laboratory in New York, many countries, including the United States, have tried to make rain. Success has been mixed.

The biggest problem in determining whether cloud seeding works is that there is no experimental control. Nobody can tell if a rain falling after a cloud-seeding experiment would have fallen anyway. There is no method of verifying the success of the experiment because scientists do not know whether the rain was due to natural causes or the experimental conditions. A study conducted in 2003 by the United States National Academy of Science was skeptical of cloud seeding, finding little proof that the process actually works. But Utah, the second-driest state in the United States (after Nevada), continues rainmaking operations in several of its regions. By examining past records, state officials say that seeding increases precipitation in these areas by 4 to 20 percent.

Even a small increase in life's most important molecule can be significant. Crops and humans need water, so if there is a way to bring it down from the atmosphere, people will try to do so. Taking advantage of the properties of this unusual polar molecule is nothing new. Condensation nuclei, hydrogen bonds, surface tension, capillary action, floating ice, and solvency combine to make H_2O an integral part of life on Earth.

4

MATERIALS

JET ENGINES POWER the fastest airplanes of today, but the first jets did not appear until the 1940s, during World War II. American inventors Wilbur and Orville Wright made the first sustained airplane flight in 1903, and all airplanes up until the development of the jet engine used slower propeller engines. The reason jets did not make an earlier appearance was not because no one had thought of the concept—people have long been familiar with jet motion, in which forward thrust comes from expelling gas or water backward at high speed. Nature uses jets, and squid propel themselves through the water in this manner. The reason jet engines did not make an earlier appearance is that no one had the right materials to make them. Jets get hot enough to melt most materials, including metals.

The jet engine is an excellent example of why materials and the physics of their structure are so important. Even the best design for an engine or structure is useless if no known material has the right properties to build it. Materials have made a huge difference in technology, as well as in the course of world history; the Greeks won their decisive victory over the invading Persian army at Marathon in 490 B.C.E. mostly because of their armor. The bronze armor worn by Greek soldiers was soft and flexible but did not break, so Persian weapons dented but did not penetrate the metal.

Some of the most critical properties of materials include strength (resistance to breaking), stiffness (resistance to twisting or bending), and ease of shaping. Different materials are made out of different elements and compounds, which gives them different properties. The three main classes of materials are metals such as copper and iron, *ceramics* such as glass, and long chains of molecules called polymers such as DNA (discussed in chapter 1) and plastic. The structure of a material is also important—a material's properties are determined by the atoms and molecules from which it is made and also how these atoms and molecules are arranged.

The properties of materials in equipment such as parachutes and cords are vitally important when lives are at stake. *(United States Air Force/2nd Lt. Shannon Collins)*

Swords, Planes, and Coins: Metals in Civilization

Metals generally have a crystalline form. The atoms of a crystal create a repeating array of a three-dimensional structure such as a cube or a hexagonal (which has a cross-section in the shape of a hexagon, a six-sided polygon). Most of the crystal contains this specific structure, repeating itself throughout the volume of the solid.

Chemists classify about 80 percent of the naturally occurring elements as metals. Common properties of metals include the ability to conduct electricity, and a solid state based on bonds called metallic bonds. The atoms of metals are closely packed together, and the bonds are strong. Metals achieve this tight packing by their atomic arrangement. Think of an atom as a hard sphere (which is not exactly true but will work as an approximation), and imagine stacking these spheres in layers inside a crate. One way to do it is by stacking the spheres directly on top of each other, forming columns as shown in part (1) of the figure on this page. But this leaves a lot of empty space between the layers. A better way is to stack a layer in the space between spheres in the lower layer, as shown in part (2) of the figure.

The most efficient use of space is the method used by most metal atoms. The layers are planes in which each sphere (atom)

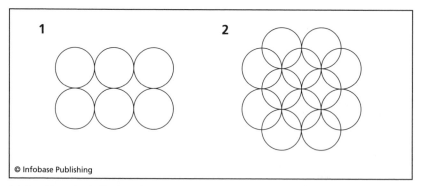

© Infobase Publishing

(1) Stacking the balls directly on top of each other forms straight columns, but there is a lot of unused space between the balls. (2) Placing the balls of one layer in the unused space of the lower layer results in a denser packing.

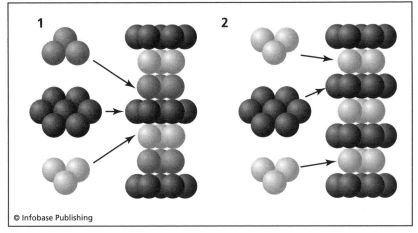

© Infobase Publishing

Two of the common atomic arrangements in metals are similar but distinct. In the first configuration, three different layers repeat to form the metal's crystal structure. An expanded view of some of the atoms is shown on the left, with arrows indicating their position in the structure. The second configuration has two different layers (the top and bottom layers of the expanded view are the same).

touches six other spheres. These layers stack upon each other by using the spaces between the spheres of the lower level, and each sphere contacts a total of 12 of its neighbors. As illustrated in the figure on this page, there are two stacking arrangements; some metals use one and some the other. In either case, this is the closest possible packing arrangement, using 74 percent of the available space.

Some materials that crystallize will form a single crystal, which repeats uniformly throughout the entire volume. Other solids tend to be composed of many crystals, separated by thin borders made up of atoms jumbled together. These solids are polycrystalline (many crystals), and the crystals are often called *grains*. Most metals are polycrystalline.

To study the structure of metals and other materials, scientists must use a variety of tools and techniques. Studying the large-scale structure of a material—the surface, for instance, and whether it is smooth or cracked—may require only an ordinary microscope, but electron microscopes provide better images. Electron microscopes send beams of electrons through a thin layer of the material or bounce electrons off the surface. Even though electrons are particles, they also have wave-like properties, and electron microscopes can form images with a great deal of detail and much higher magnification than microscopes that use light.

Examining the atomic arrangement of metals requires special instruments such as the scanning tunneling microscope (STM), as described in chapter 1, and X-ray diffraction. X-rays have a smaller wavelength than visible light and can pick out finer details. By analyzing the pattern created by X-rays as the material scatters or bends the beam, scientists can determine the structure of the crystal.

Metals are often malleable (can be hammered or pressed into sheets) and ductile (can be pulled into wires) because the atoms can roll around without breaking the strong bonds that hold them together. But the boundaries between the grains pose barriers to this movement, and the hardness of a metal depends to some extent on the number and size of its grains. Having more grains means there are more grain boundaries to restrict movement, so the metal is harder.

Armor made from layers of metal and other strong materials protects tanks such as the M1 Abrams. *(United States Army/Staff Sgt. Klaus Baesu)*

The strength and malleable nature of metal made it an extremely valuable material in ancient civilizations. Stone tools and weapons gave way to metal ones, and the Bronze Age began by about 3500 B.C.E. Ancient metalworkers heated the metal, which makes the material soft and workable. These workers soon learned that rapid cooling usually produced extremely hard objects, and slow cooling produced an object that was not quite as hard but would also not break as easily. It would bend more readily than a hard object but would be less likely to fracture under severe pressure. Cold working—hammering or beating a piece of metal while it is cold—tends to make a metal harder because it generates a lot of small grains. The following sidebar discusses the physics of the strength of materials such as metals.

People also discovered that sometimes a combination of two or more different metals produces a mixture with different properties. The combination is called an alloy. Bronze was one of the first alloys to be discovered, and is made of about 80 to 95 percent copper and the rest tin. Bronze is much harder than copper or tin alone and was used to make the best swords and armor for the armies of ancient times.

The importance of bronze in ancient times is evident in the great distances that people traveled to obtain the components. In the early civilizations of the Middle East and along the eastern regions of the Mediterranean Sea, copper was plentiful but tin was scarce. As a result, Greek and Phoenician sailors made long sea voyages to find tin. One source, located in Britain, required sailing all the way across the Mediterranean Sea, out through the Strait of Gibraltar, and into the Atlantic. To ancient mariners this was a frighteningly perilous journey.

The value and strength of metal is also shown in its use as money, a practice that has continued to the present day. No one knows for certain who minted the first coins and when, but some of the earliest coins appeared in the seventh century B.C.E. in Lydia, an area presently in Turkey. These coins consisted of a naturally occurring alloy of gold and silver called electrum. Although metal and other material had long been used for barter and trade, soon Greek and Phoenician traders began striking their own coins

Measuring the Strength of Materials

The strength of a material determines how much *stress* it can withstand. Stress is a force acting on an area, and there are three basic types—tension (stretching), *compression* (pushing together), and *shear* (twisting or sliding). *Strain* is the term used to describe the reaction of a material under stress. Physicists define tensile or compressive strain, *s*, as the change, Δl, in a material's length divided by the length, *l*, it had in the unstressed condition:

$$s = \frac{\Delta l}{l}.$$

The modulus of a material is the ratio of stress to strain or, in other words, a measurement of how much stress is required to produce a certain amount of strain. Materials with a large modulus can withstand huge forces per unit area without stretching, in the case of tension, or compacting, in the case of compression. The modulus for tensile or compressive strain is often called Young's modulus, after British physician and scientist Thomas Young (1773–1829). Shear strain measures the angle of twisting, and the shear modulus is also defined as the ratio of stress over strain.

As the stress increases, an object experiences more change (strain). If the forces are not too great then the strain is proportional to stress—a plot of stress versus strain is a straight line, as shown in the figure on page 65. This proportionality is known as Hooke's law, named for British physicist Robert Hooke (1635–1703). Under these slight stresses, a material bounces back to its original shape when the stress goes away. This behavior, called *elasticity*, results because the bonds holding together the material snap the atoms back into place upon removal of the distorting stress. But when the stress becomes too great, the bonds stretch beyond their ability to bounce back, and the material's shape changes permanently. This region of the stress/strain graph is not linear. When the stress becomes so large that the bonds fail to hold, the material breaks or fractures.

Different materials have a different modulus and elastic limits. These properties do not depend on the shape of the object but on the material—rubber is highly elastic and can stretch and bounce back by a huge amount, but the tight bonds of metals do not allow this much motion. Metals tend to be strong,

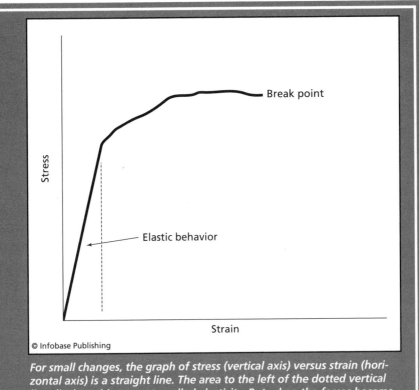

Break point

Stress

Elastic behavior

Strain

© Infobase Publishing

For small changes, the graph of stress (vertical axis) versus strain (hori-zontal axis) is a straight line. The area to the left of the dotted vertical line displays this property, called elasticity. But when the forces become too great—the exact magnitude depends on the material—the change is drastic and permanent.

though not all metals are equally strong. Lead is soft and has a Young's modulus less than a tenth of iron. Tungsten has a Young's modulus nearly twice that of iron.

Qualities other than strength and elasticity are also im-portant. To do their job, some materials must be hard—resistant to scratching or cutting—such as diamond-tipped drills that cut through dense rock or stone. Some materi-als, such as airplane parts, must be stiff so that they do not bend or change shape when subjected to air flow at high speed. The materials of the human body also have the right mix of properties for their function. Bone is a strong mate-rial and fractures less readily than concrete. This is how bones withstand the stresses of running and jumping, and is also the reason why karate experts can break a concrete cinderblock with a hand or foot.

to use as a medium of exchange. Later, the Romans made many coins from metals such as gold, silver, bronze, brass (an alloy of copper and zinc), and copper. Many Romans also admired early Greek coins and began what became a long tradition of coin collecting.

Although the value of a coin need not be tied to the value of its metallic composition, for most of its history the United States minted high-value coins from gold and minted silver or copper coins for lesser, everyday transactions. But the rising cost of these metals caused a change in the content of many coins. The nickel, dime, quarter, and half-dollar—which until 1965 were composed mostly of silver—are now mostly copper with a small amount of nickel. (The five-cent piece has about three times the nickel of the other coins but is still only 25 percent nickel.) The penny used to be copper but is now 97.5 percent zinc.

Gold is a scarce metal and valuable both because of its scarcity and the ease with which it can be fashioned into coins or ornaments. Gold is such a soft metal that coins and jewelry cannot be made from pure gold because they would be too easily damaged—a person can scratch pure gold with a fingernail. Gold coins and jewelry must be made from various alloys to increase their hardness.

One of the hardest alloys is composed of iron and an element that is not even a metal—carbon. Steel contains iron plus a small amount of carbon and plays many vital roles in today's structures. This widely used alloy will be discussed in chapter 5.

One of the most common metals today is aluminum, although it usually appears in alloy form. People did not begin using aluminum until the 19th century, but not because it is scarce—aluminum is the most abundant metal in Earth's crust, making up about 8 percent of the crust's weight. The problem was extracting aluminum. Like most metals, aluminum is almost always found in nature as part of an ore, a combination of metals or minerals. Bauxite contains aluminum, but it takes a lot of energy to extract the aluminum from the ore. This made aluminum so valuable that the only people who could afford it were royalty, who in the 1800s offered their most distinguished guests the honor of dining with aluminum knives and forks.

Although modern mining companies have lowered costs and increased the available quantity, aluminum remains expensive. Recycling is cheaper than extracting aluminum from ore, which is why aluminum is one of the most commonly recycled materials. The economy of recycling is important because aluminum is widely used today, especially in airplanes.

Airplanes must be made of strong materials that do not easily bend or break, but weight is also tremendously important. A huge amount of fuel must be burned to keep an airplane aloft, and heavier airplanes require more fuel because of their greater mass. Aluminum is about three times less dense than steel, which means it has about three times less mass than steel per unit volume. Yet aluminum is a strong material, able to resist compression. Aluminum is also able to resist shear forces arising from high-velocity travel through air—as an airplane speeds through the atmosphere, the air scrapes across the surface and will twist or distort weak materials.

For similar reasons, aluminum is also critical in space launches. Newton's second law, named after the great British physicist Sir Isaac Newton (1642–1727), states that an object's acceleration—the rate of change of its velocity—is proportional to the force acting on the object and inversely proportional to its mass. Rockets and spaceships must attain extremely high velocities in order to go into orbit or to escape Earth's gravity, and lighter structures are essential to achieve these velocities. Much of a space shuttle is made of aluminum.

Titanium is another metal that finds a lot of use in air and space travel. This element is strong and light but can also withstand high temperatures. But even titanium has trouble in the ferocious heat generated by machines such as jet engines. A jet engine continually burns fuel and uses the hot, expanding gases to push against a rotating turbine. The engine gets so hot that for many years no one knew how to make a jet engine in which the parts, especially the blades of the turbine, did not melt. Turbine blades must be made of materials called "superalloys," which contain alloys made from nickel or cobalt along with a sprinkling of other metals.

Alloys such as bronze tend to be harder than their component metals because the different atoms create distortion in the structure. Packing a set of spheres of the same size produces a uniformly smooth structure, and in a metal this means the atoms can slide past one another easily, particularly if the crystals are large so that there are few boundaries to restrict movement. But a structure composed of spheres of different sizes will have variations or lumps, and these distortions hinder the atoms' movement.

The widely varying properties of different metals and their many alloys are responsible for their many uses, but no material is perfect. Cold working a metal increases its strength by creating grain boundaries, but these boundaries are also opportunities for cracks to form. Materials tend to split along boundaries, such as wood that splits more easily when cut along the grain. (Grain in a piece of wood refers to the orientation of wood fibers, not the crystals of a metal.) Having too many boundaries can make a metal or any other material crack or break too easily. In other words, it is *brittle*. Too much cold working produces a brittle metal.

Distortions in the crystal can have similar affects. Dislocations are places where the planes of atoms are misaligned, such as in the figure on page 69, and these defects occur often in crystals (nothing in nature is perfect). If a row of atoms is missing, for example, the other rows must squeeze together. Similar to other distortions, dislocations can strengthen the material, but they also have the same disadvantages—too many will make the metal brittle.

One of the most serious problems of metals is that on occasion they break suddenly and with little warning. Metal failures have been responsible for numerous airplane accidents, including several tragedies in 1954 when two of the first jet airliners, De Havilland Comets, broke apart and crashed. Metal structures that have functioned safely for a long time can fail because the metal becomes weakened by repeated stressing, a condition known as metal fatigue. This condition is usually difficult to detect by inspection. Because of metal fatigue, engineers are wary about using a metal structure for an extended period of time.

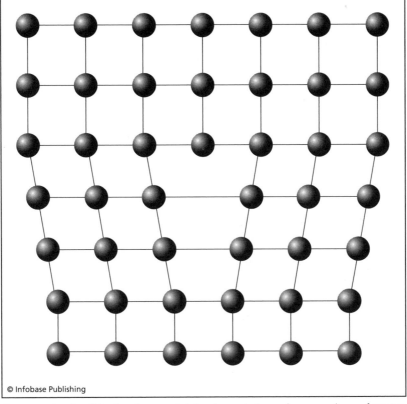

An example of a distortion in a crystal due to a missing column or plane of atoms

The advantages and disadvantages of metal make it a good choice for some applications and not for others. Metals are used not only in structures because of their strength, but also in electronics because of their electrical conductivity. Metals are good electrical conductors because their bonding creates mobile electrons, free to flow in response to applied electrical forces. All metals are good conductors, although some are better than others. Gold, silver, and copper are excellent conductors. But since gold and silver are so expensive, most wires and circuits are composed of copper.

Many other materials conduct electricity only weakly. This is advantageous when engineers need electrical insulators—materials that prevent the flow of electricity, which is necessary for control and safety purposes. High voltages can melt or break down weak insulators, so strong materials are essential for dangerous circuits. Some of the best materials for this job are ceramics, which are distinct from metals in numerous ways.

Glass and Other Ceramics

While some people always think of pottery when they hear the word *ceramics*, which derives from a Greek term referring to pottery, this class of materials includes many items made from non-metallic minerals. Common ceramics are pottery, glass, porcelain, and bricks.

Creating ceramics usually involves applying heat, sometimes called firing, to harden clay or other materials. The elements composing ceramics are some combination of metals and nonmetals, held together by strong chemical bonds. These bonds get some of their strength by tying up electrons, and because the electrons are not loose they do not flow easily, so ceramics usually make poor electrical conductors. But the strength of the material keeps it from breaking down even when a huge voltage tries to push the electrons out of their bonds, and ceramics find much use as insulators in electrical generators and transformers. Other devices involving high-voltage electricity are spark plugs, in which 20,000-volt sparks jump across a gap to ignite the fuel in internal combustion engines. One of the most common ceramics in these applications is porcelain.

In addition to their strength and insulating properties, ceramics also tend to be poor *thermal* conductors (they do not conduct heat very well) and most of them are not easily ruined by acids and other chemicals. This distinguishes them from metals, which are generally good thermal conductors and susceptible to chemical changes, especially rust. But most ceramics are similar to metals in that they are polycrystalline, although there is an important exception noted below.

Another difference between ceramics and metals is their response to stress. In most cases, metallic bonds are flexible and allow the metal to deform slightly when subjected to forces, keeping the material from breaking outright until its limit is reached. Flexible is not a word that applies to ceramics; the word best describing ceramics is brittle, because although a ceramic is hard, the material does not have a lot of give and take. Drop a metal structure on the floor and it will usually survive, even though it may pick up a dent or a bend. Drop a piece of pottery or glass on the floor and it will either stay the same or, more often, chip, crack, break, or shatter.

The properties of hardness, resistance to chemical corrosion, and thermal insulation that characterize many ceramics have led some engineers to ponder the use of ceramics in engines. Most engine parts today are made of metal but ceramics would have advantages. About a third of the heat generated by the burning fuel in car engines is wasted because it escapes by traveling through metal—even the hood of a car is hot to the touch when the engine is running. Keeping the heat inside and allowing the engine to run at even hotter temperatures would greatly increase the efficiency. Since most ceramics are not easily corroded, engines with ceramic parts would probably last longer. The lighter weight of a ceramic compared to most metals would also improve gas mileage.

The problem with ceramic engines is brittleness. A crack in the wrong spot would be enough to cause total failure of the engine, and with ceramics an engine would be one bad "knock" away from splitting. Car manufacturers Toyota and Isuzu tinkered with ceramic parts in the 1980s, but car engines made mostly or wholly of ceramics remain impossible at the present time. Despite this, researchers continue to work on ceramic engine components at laboratories such as the Glenn Research Center, a National Aeronautics and Space Administration (NASA) facility in Cleveland, Ohio, and the Air Force Research Laboratory at Wright-Patterson Air Force Base in Ohio. Lightweight ceramics have particular appeal to the weight-conscious aerospace industry.

A ceramic material presently getting a lot of use in many different devices (though not in engines) is glass. Glass differs from most ceramics because it is not generally polycrystalline. Most ordinary types of glass have little or no crystal structure at all, and are called *amorphous*. (*Morph* is a term denoting shape, and the prefix *a* means without. The positions of the glass molecules do not form a repetitive shape or structure.) Light travels through glass much more easily than other materials because glass absorbs little light and has no internal structure to scatter it.

There are many types of glass. The glass found most often today is about three-quarters silica (silicon dioxide), an abundant material found in quartz and sand. The other components are sodium carbonate and calcium oxide (lime). Glassmakers heat the material into its molten (fluid) state and shape it through various means (one of the traditional methods to shape glass involves blowing air through a tube). Then the material cools and hardens. Glassmakers must cool the glass quickly before crystals start to form, but not too quickly or the material may shatter.

As anyone who has ever dropped a glass knows, glass is brittle. This behavior is due to the bonds, similar to the reason why most ceramics are brittle. Powerful bonds hold the glass particles together but they do not stretch. In other words, a particle of glass holds onto its neighbors fiercely but only for short distances. When some force or stress is strong enough to pull glass particles apart by even a small distance, the bonds break and the material shatters.

Sometimes people call glass a supercooled liquid because it seems to have more in common with a liquid than a solid. Glass lacks internal structure and appears almost as if it is a liquid whose particles are "frozen" in random positions. This way of thinking has merit, and glass can "flow," albeit at an extremely slow rate. But the concept of a supercooled liquid can be taken too far and tends to be truer of glass when the temperature is high rather than at ordinary temperatures. For instance, after noticing that some of the windows on the old cathedrals in Europe are thicker on the bottom than the top, some people have claimed that the window glass has flowed over the centuries, settling toward the bottom because of gravity. But this is a controversial claim. Scientists such as Edgar Dutra Zanotto, from *Universidade Federal de São Carlos* (*Federal University of Sao Carlos*) in Brazil, argues that glass flows far too slowly at the temperatures to which the cathedrals are exposed. A more likely explanation in his opinion is that the glass was not uniformly smooth when it was installed.

Glass is useful not just to make windows and cups but also as thermal insulation. Homes and businesses need thermal insulation to keep the heat from escaping in the winter or the cool air from escaping in the summer. Asbestos was formerly used for insulation and fireproofing until the discovery that this material poses a health hazard, increasing the risk of some types of cancer and lung disease. A mesh of tiny glass fibers called fiberglass is currently one of the most common insulators. One of the main reasons that fiberglass is an excellent insulator is that the fibers trap air. Although glass itself is not a very good thermal conductor, air is an extremely poor conductor of heat and makes an effective insulator provided the air in fiberglass is trapped, which prevents circulation.

Sometimes people use the term *fiberglass* to refer to another type of material. This material has glass fibers embedded or glued in another substance, often plastic. This is an example of a *composite* material, which is described in a later section.

Plastic: Long Chains of Molecules

Perhaps no other material highlights the 20th and 21st centuries more than plastic. Plastic is everywhere, in wrappers and packaging, cars and airplanes, bank cards and purses. The term *plastic* comes from a Greek word *plastikos,* meaning to mold or form. Plastic can be formed and molded into any shape or size; some plastic materials are strong and rigid, some are soft and flexible, and some are between these two extremes. In the latter part of the 20th century plastic production began to exceed that of steel and aluminum combined.

Although plastic materials have a remarkable range of shape and durability, the one characteristic they all have in common is that they are polymers. A polymer is a long chain of repeating units called monomers. There are many examples of polymers found in nature. For example, DNA, discussed in chapter 1, is a polymer consisting of a chain of bonded molecules called nucleotides (to which the bases A, C, T, or G are attached). But the term *plastic* generally refers to synthetic (human-made) polymers rather than natural polymers.

Most types of plastic today are based on carbon because this element readily bonds with itself to form long chains. (Carbon is essential to much of organic chemistry and biochemistry for

Polymerization

Natural polymers such as DNA and cellulose form with the help of proteins called enzymes. Enzymes catalyze (speed up) chemical reactions but do not otherwise participate in the reaction, so they remain unchanged. In the cells of all living organisms there are enzymes called DNA polymerases that catalyze the chemical bonding of nucleotide monomers into polymers. Cellulose is a plant polymer of glucose molecules. These polymers add strength to plant tissues and form fibers used to make paper and other products. Although cellulose is made of glucose, a sugar, humans cannot digest cellulose because the enzymes necessary to break apart the bonds are not present in the human body. Another plant polymer important in industry is rubber, a polymer of a molecule called isoprene.

The process of making synthetic polymers like plastic usually begins with breaking down the hydrocarbons in petroleum with high temperatures and catalysts. This is called cracking. Large hydrocarbon molecules get broken down into smaller ones, resulting in the production of a lot of molecules like ethylene, whose structure can be seen in part (A) of the figure on page 75. (Another name for this molecule is ethene.)

Ethylene is the starting point of several different plastic materials. One of the simplest and easiest to make is a polymer of ethylene known as polyethylene. There are a number of different methods of synthesizing this plastic, and one of the most common involves highly reactive chemicals called free radicals. Free radicals have one or more unpaired electrons, which is an unstable configuration that readily enters into chemical reactions. The free radicals react with monomers such as ethylene and in the process the monomers join into a growing chain. The reactions stop when the growing ends of two chains meet, or when the end of the chain becomes capped with an atom or molecule which is "content" with its electron pairs and fails to enter into a reaction. The end products are long chains of polyethylene, as shown in part (B) of the figure on page 75.

the same reason.) Other elements are also important, particularly hydrogen. Petroleum is a rich source of hydrocarbons (compounds of carbon and hydrogen) used for making oil and gasoline, and it

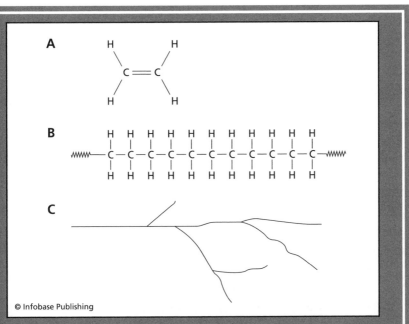

(a) The chemical structure of ethylene is simple, consisting of bonds between the hydrogen and carbon atoms and a double bond between the two carbons. Ethylene molecules bond together to form a chain or polymer, as shown in (b). These chains can be straight or they may branch, as shown in (c).

The free-radical method of synthesizing polyethylene is popular and cheap, but it produces branched polymers, shown in part (C) of the figure, rather than straight, unbranched chains. This is because free radicals will engage the carbon backbone at more than one point, in which case the chain bifurcates (splits) into two, similar to a fork in a country road.

Many types of plastic use free radicals or another method of polymerization. Chemical modifications of the monomer ethylene occurring before polymerization will result in a polymer of a different sort. For instance, replacing one of the hydrogens of ethylene with chloride generates a molecule called vinyl chloride. Polymers of this molecule are known as polyvinyl chloride and are one of the most common plastics available.

also serves as the prime ingredient for most plastic materials. Much less used are polymers based on the element silicon, although Silly Putty is a well known example. The sidebar on pages 74 and 75 describes the process of polymerization.

Manufacturers began developing the first plastics around the late 19th century, which is when the term *plastic* came into use. Inventors and researchers were motivated to investigate these new materials because they needed substances with one or more of the following properties:

1. lightweight

2. not brittle

3. not easily corroded or chemically altered

4. electrically insulating (poor conductor of electricity).

The electrical industry, which was first established around this time, had an especially urgent need of poor electrical conductors made of flexible material. Electrical circuits required such materials to keep the electricity from flowing into undesired pathways, including other circuits or metal components nearby.

Polymers had been used in various industries earlier, particularly rubber and the modification introduced by American inventor Charles Goodyear (1800–60) that vulcanizes rubber, increasing its durability. But rubber is a natural polymer and not generally called a plastic (although today there are synthetic rubber substances which many people classify as plastics).

One of the earliest plastics was celluloid, a material made by treating the plant polymer cellulose with chemicals. Photographic film made of celluloid strips became extremely popular in the early 20th century, and most of the early movies are made from it. But celluloid degrades over time and is not used for film anymore. The old celluloid movies have deteriorated so badly that they are now in dismal shape.

Another early plastic was Bakelite, invented by Leo Baekeland (1863–1944), a Belgian chemist who came to live in the United States. Many people consider Bakelite the first "true" plastic because it was a purely synthetic material made with chemicals called phenol and formaldehyde. Bakelite performed a large number of functions in the electrical industry and rapidly found its way in kitchens and dining rooms as various containers and utensils.

As the usefulness of plastic became apparent, manufacturers began to develop many different types. Polystyrene was an early type of plastic that became important in containers and utensils as well as becoming the basis of another material, made by allowing air to bubble through polystyrene as it forms. This material is known as Styrofoam, popularly used in cups, particularly those intended for use with hot beverages. (The trapped air is a good thermal insulator, as mentioned earlier.) Teflon is a plastic also known as polytetrafluoroethylene, and it makes excellent stick-free coatings, among other uses.

Another important plastic is polyvinyl chloride. This material went into making the old vinyl records, which stored music and played it back on turntable record players. Vinyl records were replaced by cassette tapes, which in turn have been mostly replaced by compact discs (CDs), but polyvinyl chloride has found many other uses. Today most credit cards and other bank cards—"plastic money"—are made from polyvinyl chloride.

Polyethylene is another inexpensive and abundant plastic. It formed most of the plastic used by businessman Earl Tupper in his highly successful Tupperware containers, and today finds many additional uses in packaging, electrical insulation, and bottles. A common use of polyethylene is the plastic grocery bag. When a grocery clerk asks "Paper or plastic?" the plastic option is most likely polyethylene. Manufacturers make more than a trillion of these bags annually.

The durability and resistance to chemical change of most plastics has a negative side, however. This is well illustrated in the case of polyethylene bags. People throw away many of those trillions of bags, and instead of degrading and disappearing, these bags clog dump sites, litter the streets, or become wound around fence posts.

Litter is not the only problem created by enduring and improperly discarded plastic materials. Animals may ingest these materials by mistake and find themselves unable to clear their throats or stomachs of the material. Birds and sea animals such as marine turtles, dolphins, and whales are common victims. On other occasions, animals may become entangled in plastic sheets or strips, unable to free themselves. The Whale and Dolphin Conservation Society (WDCS), an organization devoted to the welfare of these marine mammals, reports that an estimated 100,000 marine mammals die every year from plastic ingestion or entanglement. The WDCS has noted a number of cases of whale deaths, including one in August 2000, found at Trinity Bay, Australia. An examination showed the whale's stomach contained no food but was instead clogged with plastic from grocery bags, packages, several large sheets, and various other fragments.

Part of the solution to this problem is to encourage and more strongly enforce antilittering laws. Recycling plastic is an economic incentive, and it is much more fruitful than tossing plastic on the roadway or the sea, or allowing the material to sit uselessly at dump sites. Many communities today have plastic recycling programs.

Although recycling is an excellent method of disposal, for many types of plastic it is not particularly economic because the product is so cheap to manufacture. An alternative solution to the disposal problem is to make plastics more easily degradable. This solution would entail altering the chemical structure of the polymers to make them more, rather than less, susceptible to chemical degradation. Polyethylene grocery bags endure for a decade or two before finally decomposing, and many types of plastic bottles may last billions of years, all the way through the remainder of Earth's history. (This is not an exaggeration!)

There are several avenues to making plastics degradable or "biodegradable" (which refers to the process by which certain organisms such as bacteria accelerate the breakdown of a material). One way of making plastic biodegradable is to base it on starch rather than petroleum; starch is a polymer of glucose and is a favorite food for many microorganisms. Numerous plastics manufacturers have developed starch-based plastics, but these materials have yet to gain widespread usage because they are more expensive than petroleum plastics. Other companies, such as DuPont, are researching water-soluble forms of plastic, which would degrade a lot quicker than the current products.

Even though the durability of plastics has a negative aspect, these materials are so adaptable and beneficial that they will continue to be used, in one form or another, for a long time to come. Plastics fill an enormous number of jobs all by themselves and play an even greater number of roles when combined with other material. Materials called composites, discussed below, often contain plastic in conjunction with another substance.

Synthetic Fibers

A special function that some types of plastic perform involves thin fibers. Textile manufacturers have long used natural fibers such as flax, wool, silk, and cotton to make clothes and rugs, but these fibers can sometimes be expensive and scarce, depending on the year's harvest. And while textiles made with these nature-made fibers have desirable qualities of warmth and softness, other human-made fibers can often do as well or better. Around 1900, while physicists began accumulating theoretical and practical knowledge of molecules, as discussed in the previous chapters, inventors and chemists turned their attention to duplicating or improving upon natural materials. The results include the plastics described above and a number of synthetic polymer fibers.

The earliest human-made fiber was rayon, developed in the late 19th century. Although some people do not consider rayon a synthetic fiber because it was made from wood pulp, a natural material rich in cellulose, it was not a natural fiber. Rayon is not common today, but for many years it served as an alternative to cotton. Although slightly more expensive than cotton, rayon's versatility allowed it to be used in a number of different fabrics.

The first synthetic, plastic fiber was nylon, developed by DuPont and introduced in 1938. Some people claim the term *nylon* derives from the initials of New York, where the material made one of its first appearances, but no one knows for certain how nylon got its name. Made from molecules derived from coal, nylon is a polymer having several varieties differing in the chemistry of the linkages between its components. One of the first uses of nylon was in women's stockings (hosiery). Nylon stockings are strong, sheer, and as soft as silk, but more affordable. World War II interrupted the production of nylon stockings during the early 1940s, and when manufacturers reintroduced this product, the demand was so great that riots took place in stores unable to fill all their customers' orders.

The most common method of manufacturing synthetic fibers such as nylon is known as extrusion. The polymer initially needs to have a consistency similar to a thick solution of honey, so if the material is solid, the manufacturer must either melt or dissolve it before extrusion. The process of extrusion forces the fluid through a device called a spinnerette, which has one or more small holes and resembles a showerhead. The extruded material solidifies, forming thin fibers. As the synthetic fibers solidify (and sometimes afterward), manufacturers often subject the material to tension. What this accomplishes is a further alignment of the fiber's molecules, which orients them in the axial (lengthwise) direction and tends to increase the *tensile strength*. Such fibers are stronger and more resistant to breakage.

Nylon products have been around for nearly 70 years, and the material is still commonly found in toothbrushes, stockings, fishing lines, strings, and other objects. Another important synthetic fiber is polyester, a polymer of a chemical group known as esters. (Some natural polyesters also exist, although the word generally refers to the synthetic variety.) Polyesters are widely found in clothing, either alone or blended with cotton. Other synthetic fibers include acrylic, spandex (which makes elastic, rubberlike fabrics), and polyolefin.

Many people considered clothing made from synthetic fibers to be less comfortable when these fabrics first appeared, and a lot of people still prefer natural fabrics made from cotton, wool, or silk. But the development of synthetic fibers expanded the number of available textiles, providing a variety of choices suitable for all purposes and occasions. Not only clothing but also carpets, mats, and other products could be produced. Modern fabrics are often blends of different materials, including natural and synthetic fibers.

Clothing made from synthetic fibers usually lasts longer than natural fabrics, and they tend to be more resilient, needing less ironing because they are less prone to wrinkling. When the author of this book enlisted in the United States Air Force, the supply sergeant gave him and his fellow airmen uniforms that were either cotton or polyester. Some airmen got cotton, some got polyester, and like many assignments in the military, it was the luck of the draw which one they got. The airmen with polyester uniforms, which included the author, could relax at night and watch the airmen with cotton uniforms toil away in the barracks with an iron, pressing their uniform for the next day.

Most synthetic fibers come from petroleum products, as do many plastics. But more environmentally friendly and sometimes even degradable fibers have started to make an appearance, such as a material called Ingeo™. NatureWorks LLC, a company based in Minnetonka, Minnesota, makes this fiber from corn by a process of extrusion. Corn may seem to be a strange choice, but the sugars in cornstarch provide workable material well suited for this purpose, and corn is one of the most abundant crops in the world. (Other plants, such as soybeans and alfalfa, have too much oil or protein to be as effective as corn.) Only renewable resources go into making Ingeo, unlike petroleum-based fibers, and Ingeo fibers are readily degradable, similar to natural fibers such as cotton or wool.

The type and variety of synthetic fibers are limited by nothing except the physics and chemistry of materials and the imagination of the designers. One type of fiber has even been useful in saving lives by stopping bullets.

Kevlar and Bulletproof Vests

Stephanie Kwolek, a research scientist working for DuPont, created a remarkable synthetic material in 1965. It is nearly five times stronger than an equal weight of steel. After DuPont scientist Herb Blades developed a method in 1970 to produce a large quantity of

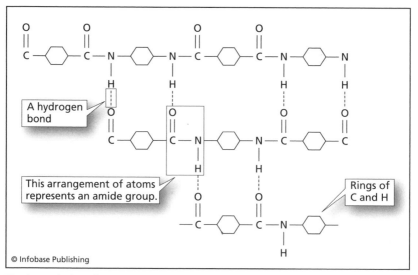

The long chains of aromatic rings and amide groups of Kevlar join together with hydrogen bonds, making an exceptionally strong material.

fibers made from this material, DuPont began to sell and market products based on it. The company called the material Kevlar.

Kevlar is a type of polymer known as a polyaromatic amide. The polymer's long chains include rings of a type known as an aromatic group, and a chemical group called amide, composed of carbon, hydrogen, oxygen, and nitrogen atoms. The strength of fibers made of Kevlar comes from the orientation and bonding among these atoms.

The polymer chains composing the fiber are parallel, like the long, thin wires of a cable. Hydrogen bonds among the amide groups hold the polymer strands tightly together. Although these bonds, as discussed in chapter 1, are relatively weak, there are many of them in these fibers. The aromatic rings, as revealed by instruments that use X-rays to image the molecular arrangement of the material, give Kevlar fibers a rigid, repeating structure that is symmetric and well ordered—a crystal. This precise internal ordering results in a strong structure, with few weak spots where the material can break. The aromatic rings and their configuration is one of the main reasons for the amazing strength of Kevlar fibers.

The proper orientation of the polymers does not occur naturally. As is the case with the other synthetic fibers discussed above, manufacturers employ the extrusion method to make Kevlar fibers. The dissolved material extrudes from the spinnerette, and after processing the polymers adopt the crystalline structure. Material used in the making of fabrics must be pure, since contaminant molecules may squeeze in between the spaces of the structure and dangerously weaken the polymer bonding.

One of the earliest applications of Kevlar was bulletproof vests. These vests form what is known as soft body armor, "soft" because it is wearable attire, not an inflexible piece of metal. A hard, metallic piece of armor stops bullets by deflecting them, but the Kevlar vests stop bullets by "catching" them in a web of many layers of fabric, woven together. Unless the bullet is from a high-power weapon, it is unable to penetrate the fiber, and the material absorbs some of the impact energy. The rest of the energy transfers to the wearer of the vest, causing a certain amount of bruising, but this is much less severe than a wound made by a bullet's entry. Kevlar vests need to be waterproofed, since the polar molecules of water can interfere with the bonds holding together the fiber's polymers.

Although Kevlar cannot protect the wearer from every potential threat, the vests do an excellent job of preventing serious injury from knives and small- and medium-caliber guns. DuPont, the manufacturer, reports that in 25 years of widespread use, Kevlar vests have saved the lives or decreased the severity of injuries of more than 2,700 police officers. The material also resists fire, succumbing only to temperatures greater than 840°F (450°C), so it offers protection against extreme temperatures resulting from flames or explosions.

The military also uses Kevlar "armor" to protect their personnel. Kevlar applications include vests, helmets, gloves, boots, blankets, and suits. In the United States, Personnel Armor System Ground Troops (PASGT) gear made with Kevlar has protected soldiers since the early 1980s, and newer gear such as the advanced combat helmet, also made of Kevlar, have also appeared. Kevlar vests and helmets offer exceptional protection against shrapnel

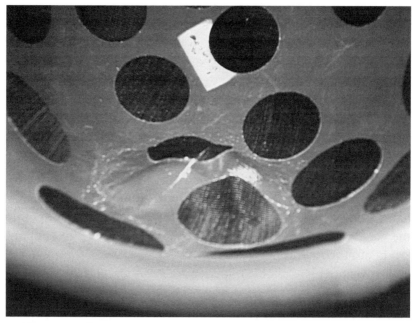

Staff Sergeant Shannon West was wearing this advanced combat helmet when it was struck by a fragment from an explosion. West survived because the Kevlar helmet, though dented, stopped the fragment. *(United States Army)*

(high-speed fragments from an exploding shell), and have been widely used in the recent Afghanistan and Iraq conflicts; Kevlar helmets offer 25 to 40 percent more protection than the formerly used steel "pots." This invaluable service is due to the physics of atoms and materials, as well as to the researchers who made the discoveries.

Kevlar finds other uses in sports equipment, protective gear for animal handlers, sails, parachutes, and as components of airplanes and helicopters. In some applications, manufacturers glue Kevlar fibers to another type of material. This process produces a composite—a material made from several different components.

Composite Materials

Composites are some of the most widely used materials in the world today. Most of these composites consist of fibers of some kind glued to another material, called the matrix. Fibers used in composites include glass, carbon, Kevlar, and others, while common matrix materials are plastic, ceramic, and metal.

Fibers add stiffness, similar to the manner by which a paintbrush's bristles, while flexible, are stiff. The fibers used in most composites are usually thin and short, and with these small sizes they can be extremely tough and strong. The job of the matrix is to bind and support the fibers, holding them together and protecting the individual filaments. Cracks are less likely in the material because of the strength of the fibers, which are embedded in the surrounding matrix. Although metal or ceramic is sometimes used as the matrix, plastic is often the ideal choice since it is light in weight, provides excellent adherence and binds the fibers tightly, and is easy to form into a variety of shapes. A negative aspect of a plastic matrix is that it adds weight but generally does not add a great deal of strength, so most applications use as little material as possible. A typical composite may have a third of its weight in the matrix.

Sometimes people call all types of composite materials "plastic." Although the term *plastic* refers to polymers, as discussed above, the reliance on plastic as the matrix for many kinds of composites means that this usage of the term is not entirely wrong.

But composites are not simply plastic, and they exist in nature as well as in technology. Bone is a composite material. The matrix of bone consists of protein molecules called collagen, which is a polymer of amino acids, as are all proteins. Embedded within the collagen matrix are small crystals of a mineral called hydroxyapatite. This mineral contains calcium, phosphate, oxygen, and hydrogen, and its presence adds strength to the bone. A loss of calcium, as sometimes occurs in old age or to astronauts who experience long periods in an orbiting spacecraft, results in significant weakening of bone. Another natural composite is wood, which contains cellulose fibers in a rigid matrix of a material called lignin. Wood has long been one of the best and widest used materials, as discussed in the following chapter.

Although many people think of synthetic composites as modern materials, the idea is not a new one. Thousands of years ago people built homes with composite bricks, made of clay or dried mud and straw. Adding the straw formed a better material than the mud alone because it was less susceptible to cracks. These bricks were strong but were not too brittle, avoiding the unfortunate tendency to crack or split that characterizes many types of brick and other ceramic material. The straw was similar to the fibers of modern composite materials, and the mud was the matrix. Then, as now, the combination of materials in a composite produces a substance with superior properties.

Archers in ancient times in Asia have also made use of composites. A string attached to a piece of wood makes a fine bow, and when the archer pulls an arrow on the string and releases it, the stretched string and wood snaps back and sends the arrow flying away at high speed. Some creative archers realized that animal sinews have excellent strength under tension, so they included this material in their bows. (Sinews are the tendons with which the muscles attach to bone.) By gluing sinews to a piece of hardwood or horn, these archers made stronger, more durable bows that could impart a huge amount of energy to an arrow.

With the development of plastics in the early 20th century, the use of synthetic material became more frequent. Glass manufacturers began making glass fiber for a variety of purposes in the 1930s, since thin fibers of glass are quite strong. When researchers discovered that the addition of such fibers to a matrix of plastic added strength and yielded an excellent product, the use of composites became popular. As the 1930s and 1940s progressed, a material called fiberglass gained widespread usage in fixtures, wall panels, and boat hulls. Fiberglass is made of glass fibers embedded in a plastic (polymer) matrix and is a material with a highly useful combination of strength and light weight. This composite gradually replaced wood and metal as the traditional material for small boats, with the advantage that, when exposed to water, fiberglass does not rot like wood or rust like metal. During World War II, the Allies invaded German-occupied France on D-Day, June 6, 1944, landing a huge number of troops and supplies carried in part by ships made with fiberglass.

A more general name for fiberglass is glass fiber reinforced plastics (GFRP). Car manufacturers soon turned to GFRPs, and in the 1950s the streamlined Corvette, with its fiberglass body, made its appearance. Fiberglass, with its strength, lightness, and the ease in which it can be maintained, was a wise choice for this longtime favorite sports car. The applications for GFRPs grew to include electrical equipment, helicopter blades, and firearms. GFRPs were not only the earliest popular composite materials, but also they are still probably the most widely used.

Another item on the list of objects replaced by composites is the shiny chrome bumper on automobiles. Cars in the 1950s and earlier often displayed a prominent amount of chrome in the front and back. Although a number of motorists felt that the polished metal added a certain amount of beauty and dignity to the machine—and there are still people who yearn for this old style of automobile—the bumpers were heavy and difficult for the manufacturers to shape. Plastic material or composites offered significant savings in weight, which increased gas mileage since lighter cars do not use as much fuel.

Another important advantage is that plastics and composites can be molded, forming the desired shape in the process of being made. Metal is more difficult to hammer into shape. The easily molded plastic or composite material gave engineers who design cars the freedom to consider all manner of styles, and the manufacturing process permitted the bumpers to become a part of the car rather than something that was stuck on as an afterthought. A metal bumper was a separate item that must be attached or welded to the car's frame, whereas a composite bumper could be fit into any desirable style. Cars may have lost their chrome dignity, but they gained elegance as well as an increase in gas mileage.

The aerospace industry was not far behind. Weight is an extremely important consideration for airplanes and space vehicles, for the same reason as cars—heavier craft require more fuel and increase operating expenses. As previously mentioned, this weight "penalty" is particularly troubling in space launches. Unnecessary weight increases the amount of fuel needed to reach the high speeds of orbit or escape velocity (the speed necessary to escape

Earth's gravity), and this extra fuel adds even more mass, worsening the problem.

But fiberglass is not quite strong and light enough for aerospace applications. Fiberglass also cannot withstand the high temperatures associated with the exceptional speeds of airplanes and rockets. Engineers turned to newer fibers made of carbon, boron, a compound called silicon carbide, or Kevlar, and embedded these fibers in a matrix of ceramic or metal. Fibers made of carbon became increasingly important in composites, thanks to their low cost and excellent stiffness and strength.

The use of metal as a matrix material adds weight, but such material can also withstand heat without unacceptable weakening or expansion. Thermal expansion is an expansion of volume with a rise in temperature and is a property that virtually all materials experience to a greater or lesser extent. A metal-matrix composite (MMC) tends not to expand as much with increasing temperature. Expansion of the components of a vehicle in flight can be disastrous, as the frame or structure may be weakened to the point of failure.

An earlier section of this chapter described the use of aluminum in airplanes and space vehicles, and the metal also makes an effective matrix for MMCs. Rocket and spaceship components,

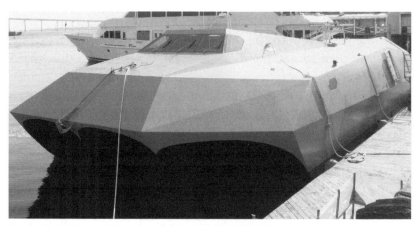

The hull of this experiment vessel is made from carbon composites, strong enough to withstand the pounding of waves during high-speed maneuvering. *(Department of Defense/Samantha L. Quigley)*

including parts of the engine and body, are frequently composed of aluminum reinforced with carbon or silicon carbide fibers.

Another valuable addition to the list of composite materials is sometimes referred to as a carbon-carbon composite. The fiber of these materials is often graphite, a form of carbon also used in pencils and for lubrication. Carbon is an element having a variety of different forms, and the matrix of a carbon-carbon composite is also carbon, but with a different structure. These materials have excellent properties, including strength and the ability to withstand extreme temperatures.

The light weight and strength of composites are not the only advantages over metal. Composites experience little fatigue, a property of metals that as discussed earlier has caused a number of disastrous accidents. By using composites, air- and spacecraft can be light, strong, and durable. The amazingly light *Voyager,* made solely of composites and piloted by Dick Rutan and Jeana Yeager, circled the globe nonstop in 1986. Try that with a metal airplane! Composites form the bulk of the shell of many types of race cars as well as the body of *SpaceShipOne,* the vehicle that won the $10 million Ansari X Prize in 2004. *SpaceShipOne,* built by a company called Scaled Composites and piloted by a single flier (either Michael Melvill or Brian Binnie), won the prize by making the first privately funded space launch. The vehicle reached an altitude of 62 miles (100 km) twice within a two-week period.

Despite the advantages of composites, the big jets flown by airlines and made by companies such as Boeing and Airbus are mostly aluminum. The Boeing 777, for example, is made of 50 percent aluminum and only 12 percent composite by weight. This is in contrast to the more recent fighter jets of the United States Air Force, which generally consist of a higher percentage of composite material. About a third of the weight in the structure of the F-22 Raptor, the latest fighter jet, is composite.

The reason that military jets make a higher use of composites than the airlines is due to economics. Airlines are in the business of transporting people from place to place in order to make a profit (although most of these companies have not been very successful in recent times). Aluminum is usually heavier than composite and adds to the fuel bill, but aluminum structures are generally cheaper and do not cost as much in maintenance.

The U.S. Air Force has different goals. A fighter pilot's life may depend on a speedy maneuver, and, in this situation, an airplane that is sluggish from any extra weight it is carrying can be deadly. The military prefers to pay more for its jets and the cost of maintaining them if these airplanes can help preserve the lives of their pilots.

But with advances in the physics and engineering of materials, not only do new materials become available, but also their cost tends to drop. This is true of many technologies—the price of computers has dropped considerably as engineers develop better and cheaper components and manufacturing processes. And with the increased use of composites, designers have become more comfortable and skilled with using this class of material.

The advantages of composites recently prompted Boeing to reduce the amount of aluminum for their new model, the 787 "Dreamliner." The 787, scheduled to make its first flight in 2007, will be 50 percent composite, 20 percent aluminum, 15 percent titanium, 10 percent steel, and 5 percent other materials. Although Boeing has not yet started manufacturing this airplane, they have begun to take advance orders from the airlines and have been pleased with the number of sales. The pricetag, $120 million, compares favorably to other models of a similar size, and the advantages are many. Boeing says that the 787 will be about 20 percent more fuel efficient than comparable planes. The strength and resistance to corrosion of composites will allow the cabin to hold a greater air pressure and increase the size of windows, giving passengers a more comfortable and superior sightseeing ride.

Shielding a Space Shuttle: Heat-resistant Tiles

A difficulty with any material on high-speed craft, whether made of aluminum or composite, is heat. Friction is a force caused by the rubbing of one object on another, and a vehicle moving in air encounters friction as the air molecules hit and rub against its surface. This process, as in all friction, raises the temperature of the surface. At the tremendous velocities with which many vehicles travel today, friction becomes so great that the temperature rises to a dangerous level.

An especially difficult situation occurs when an orbiting space-craft reenters Earth's atmosphere, although the process is not the same as frictional heating. Spacecraft such as satellites orbit above the atmosphere so that there is no air to slow the high speeds they need to stay in orbit. But if the orbiting object needs to return to Earth, as is the case with a space shuttle and its crew of astronauts, the vehicle must of course travel through the atmosphere to make a landing. The danger is that an orbiting vehicle must have so much speed to stay in orbit—a space shuttle's orbital velocity is about 17,300 miles per hour (27,680 km/h)—and these speeds generate extreme temperatures when the vehicle must travel through air. Special material must protect the surface from the effects of heating.

A space shuttle's main problem on reentry is not friction, since at the time of reentry the vehicle is at the top of the atmosphere, where the air is quite thin. Friction is a serious concern in the dense air of the lower atmosphere, but by the time the shuttle reaches this altitude it is not going nearly as fast as during reentry. The heating of reentry is due mostly to the intense air pressure waves created by the high-speed motion of the large body of the shuttle. As the shuttle enters the atmosphere it still has much of its orbital velocity, and it hits the air molecules with so much force that it causes many of them to break apart. This process creates an ionized gas called a plasma, a state of matter discussed in chapter 2. This hot plasma can raise the surface temperature of the reentry vehicle to 2,300°F (1,260°C).

The heat generated by reentry is actually a necessary part of a space shuttle's return. The shuttle must lose most of its orbital velocity in order to land, but it has no brakes. One possible method of braking would be to use a jet to provide reverse thrust, which would be similar to a rocket engine pointing backward, but this method would require the shuttle to carry a significant amount of extra fuel. This fuel would increase the shuttle's mass and elevate the cost of launch, as well as requiring the shuttle to carry a dangerous amount of fuel during its orbit. The shuttle has a little fuel during reentry to power the small engines it uses for maneuvering, but it does not use its engines for braking. Instead, the shuttle slows down by expending its energy in creating the hot plasma and, especially at lower altitudes, losing energy due to friction.

Protecting exposed surfaces from high temperature are a set of about 25,000 thermal or heat-resistant tiles. Temperatures greater than 350°F (177°C) can damage the aluminum frame of a shuttle, so the tiles must be able to sustain exceptionally hot temperatures on one side while remaining much cooler on the other. A variety of different types of tiles cover the shuttle's surface, but the tiles covering the leading edges and underside of the craft must resist the highest temperatures. High-temperature Reusable Surface Insulation (HRSI) tiles consist of extremely pure silica (the same material in sand) and have an exceptionally low density. These tiles have a thickness of about 1 to 5 inches (2.5–12.5 cm), thicker at the front of the vehicle and thinnest near the rear. An HRSI tile sheds heat at such a phenomenal rate that a person can hold one with bare hands even if the tile was in a 2,300°F (1,260°C) oven

This view of the thermal tiles of the space shuttle *Discovery*'s underside was photographed during an extravehicular activity on August 3, 2005. *(NASA/ Stephen K. Robinson)*

a few seconds earlier. Another tile, Fibrous Refractory Composite Insulation (FRCI), adds fibers to the silica, which improves the strength and durability.

Attaching these tiles to a shuttle's surface is not simply a matter of gluing them on the aluminum frame. The aluminum encounters heat during the flight of the vehicle, and while the temperature increase is endurable, thanks to the tiles, the metal gets hot enough to expand. But the thermal tiles do not expand as much, and they are too brittle to withstand the volume change experienced by the metal. Firmly attaching the tiles to the aluminum would result in their cracking and falling off as the frame expanded. Instead, the manufacturer mounts the tiles on a flexible felt pad, with gaps filled by a compressible rubbery material. The gap fillers usually go unnoticed, but during a 2005 mission of the space shuttle *Discovery,* several gap fillers accidentally protruded from the surface. NASA scientists worried that the protrusions would cause increased heating during reentry, so astronaut Stephen Robinson ventured outside of the orbiting vehicle and removed the gap fillers.

Prosthetics: Artificial Body Parts

The special thermal properties of a shuttle's tiles protect the vehicle from high temperatures. This is one of the main advantages of materials such as plastics and composites—engineers and scientists can employ their knowledge of the physics and chemistry of materials to create new and unique substances to fill specific roles. The required properties can vary widely, depending on the function and structure of the object. When the object is a prosthesis—an artificial body part—the critical properties prove to be similar to aerospace applications.

Artificial (prosthetic) limbs, which are one type of prosthesis, are fortunately not as common as they were in the past. Before the development of antibiotics in the 20th century, many injuries, even if only moderate, resulted in infections that necessitated removal of the affected limb. Soldiers receiving war injuries were particularly vulnerable, and thousands of veterans from both sides of the

American Civil War came home missing an arm or leg. Amputees often wore wood or metal replacements, which were bulky, awkward, and sometimes impeded rather than aided motion.

Even with the improved medicine of today, estimates of the number of amputees in the United States alone approach one million. But the modern science of materials provides a vastly improved set of prosthetic limbs, and the mobility of the most athletic amputees approaches that of non-amputees. Marlon Shirley, a leg amputee, has run the 100-meter dash in 11.08 seconds, only about a second behind the fastest Olympic sprinter.

Athletic feats such as Shirley's are amazing considering the effort required to walk or run with an artificial leg. Prosthetic legs can weigh 5 or more pounds (22 N), and since there are no muscles in the limb to move it—and usually no other devices either—the wearer must supply all the energy. Walking can take one and a half times the normal effort.

To lighten the load, prosthetic limb manufacturers use lightweight material. Yet the limb must be strong as well as light, particularly for legs, since they must support the body's weight and endure the pounding that occurs while the person is walking or running. Wood and metal such as steel are strong, durable materials, but they are also heavy. Aluminum and titanium are better choices, offering a combination of strength and light weight.

Newer prosthetic limbs make use of composites. Carbon fiber composites, materials that aerospace engineers and scientists developed for airplanes and spacecraft applications, perform splendidly in this role. As is true of NASA's vehicles, people want to travel lightly and quickly, wasting as little energy as possible in the process. Composites are easy to move, yet strong enough to withstand the rigors of strenuous activity.

German athlete and amputee Wojtek Czyz is an excellent example. Czyz won three gold medals in the 2004 Paralympics, which is a highly competitive set of contests for disabled persons, held at the same time and place as the Olympics. Considering the skill of Czyz, Shirley, and many of the other athletes, the word *disabled* does not really apply, for these athletes sprint, jump, and maneuver as well as anybody. Moving this vigorously subjects the person to tremendous forces, particularly in the joints, and Czyz's left leg prosthesis had to be extremely tough. Materials used in his artificial limb came directly from the European Space Agency's efforts, and each of the contests in which Czyz participated placed a different set of requirements on the limb. For sprints, the prosthesis needed a bracket made from special aluminum alloys, but for long jumps, a bracket of carbon composite was the better choice. The composite permitted a layering of the material that was stiff enough to withstand the crushing force of landing during long jump events.

Improvements in prosthetics have helped a wide range of people. Hip replacements are common because hips experience a lot of stress over a lifetime, but the prosthetic implant must be strong to survive this same stress. Composites made with silicon carbide fibers result in hip implants that are about one and a half times as strong as the previous ceramic or metal implants.

But metal is not without its uses in modern prosthetics. Titanium offers excellent strength at a relatively light weight and is commonly used for implanted devices or objects, such as plates or screws to hold broken bones in place while they mend. Titanium has a tremendous advantage over many other materials when used as an implant because this metal is remarkably biocompatible—it does not react with the body. The tissues of the body are about 70 percent water in terms of weight, and this water contains a considerable amount of ions, making it "salty." Such an environment is ideal for rust and corrosion, limiting the type of material that can be used in the body. Titanium resists these effects exceptionally well and does not interact in any other harmful way with the body's cells and tissues. This makes titanium a splendid metal for implants of all kinds.

Materials of the Future

Metals and their alloys remain useful for a variety of purposes, and the use of plastics and composites, whose composition can be engineered to suit an even wider variety of purposes, will continue to increase. But despite the versatility of plastics and composites, most of these materials have limits. One of the biggest limits is that they are static—once mixed, shaped, and fit into place, a static material does not change.

A lack of change would not seem to be associated with any disadvantages. A rigid structure, for instance, must remain strong, allowing no weakening that could lead to collapse. But the stresses on an object can and often do change during its use, and the varying conditions put varying demands on the material. A static material does not change, and so its properties must meet the demands of any possible condition. This will often result in compromises—to fulfill widely varying demands, a material generally cannot be ideal for all of them. As in apparel, one size does not fit all.

Responding to change relies on a certain degree of adaptability. Although there are certainly limits, animals and people excel at adapting to their environment. For instance, people move in a number of different ways, depending on whether they are moving uphill or downhill, and moving with a wind to their back or struggling to make progress against a fierce gust. These different movements require activation of differing sets of muscles, which maintain upright posture and propel the person forward. Bodies are not static, they are dynamic, changing positions and movements to suit the environment. Another way of saying this is that people are smart—they do not dumbly apply the same strategy to all conditions.

Future materials will probably be more adaptable than the unchanging materials of today. In the coming years, materials will become "smart." Current research on smart materials engages a broad range of applications, but one of the most prominent examples is flight.

During flight, an airplane experiences a variety of conditions and stresses. American inventors and brothers Wilbur and Orville Wright accomplished the earliest significant flight in 1903, using an airplane they controlled by adjusted the shape of the wings. Air flowing over the wings provides an airplane with a lifting force, due at least in part to the shape of the wing—the air flowing over the upper surface moves faster than the air flowing underneath, which by Bernoulli's principle means that the pressure is greater underneath the wing, creating a lifting force. The wings also stabilize the airplane, maintaining a steady, even course. To maintain stability during the varying conditions of flight, the wings must be adjustable, somewhat like a tightrope walker swaying his or her arms, or an extended pole, to keep balanced. The Wright brothers designed their airplane such that they could adjust the wings as necessary by twisting them.

Although the Wright brothers' airplane flew, it was slow. Designers soon began putting more powerful engines on their airplanes, making them go increasingly faster. The faster speeds subjected the wings to a lot more stress than they previously had experienced. In order to withstand these stresses, wings had to become stronger and stiffer. This rigidity prevented airplane designers from using adjustable wings, as such wings would be torn apart at high speeds. Instead, airplane wings made any essential alterations with the aid of movable panels firmly attached to their edges or surfaces. The pilot adjusts panels such as the flaps and ailerons in order to change the airflow over and around the wings. Such adjustment permits pilots to turn the plane, change altitude, or manipulate the lifting force as needed during takeoffs and landings.

Rigid wings and movable panels are a compromise. They are stiff enough to endure forces created by high speeds, but they also add weight and complexity to the airplane as well as increase air resistance. These panels became necessary because no one knew of any material that could withstand a huge amount of stress and yet bend or twist like the wings of the Wright brothers' plane.

But as materials research advances, flexible yet strong materials are emerging, along with newer methods of controlling them. A recent project involving NASA, the Air Force Research Laboratory, and engineers from Boeing has studied jet wings that twist and warp to provide stability and control, similar to the old Wright brothers' airplane. This project, called Active Aeroelastic Wing (AAW), uses a special F/A-18 Air Force jet. The original design of the wings of this jet had been rejected because they were too flexible, causing undesirable twisting during high-speed maneuvers. Now engineers realize that if they can control the twisting, they can use these movements to their advantage, adjusting the wing to meet the varying conditions from moment to moment.

The AAW jet still has movable panels such as flaps and ailerons, but these panels merely support the adjustments made by the morphing (reshaping) wing. The AAW wing shows elasticity, the ability to snap back into place after changing shape, and it does so actively (on purpose), rather than as a passive response to stress. The morphing wing reshapes itself to adjust the airflow, accomplishing what the stiff, movable panels are intended to do. Controlling the reshaping process are surfaces at the leading and trailing edges of the wing, governed by a computer system. The

An experimental F/A-18A, modified for the Active Aerolastic Wing project, performs a roll. (NASA/Jim Ross)

wings use the energy of the airflow itself to help warp the surface as needed.

Although this technology is not fully developed, its potential advantages are many. If wings can dispense with movable panels, or at least make do with much smaller ones, they can be 10 to 20 percent lighter than conventional wings and reduce air resistance. The thin, flexible wings could also lead to reductions in the weight and complexity of the rest of the airplane, whose surfaces and structure must often support the function and performance of the wings.

The wings of the AAW F/A-18 are composed of a combination of aluminum and composites. Using a variety of materials in a structure, instead of making it from a single substance, adds complexity to the design but also permits a greater range of possibilities. And researchers have only just begun investigating the full number of possibilities and combinations.

Shape-changing wings are not entirely new, even in the recent era. For instance, the B1B and F-14, two military aircraft, have the ability to sweep their wings back and forth. But these movements are not nearly as effective as the type of movement made by a peregrine falcon, one of the world's fastest birds. The best shape for a wing differs considerably when the bird is soaring with the air currents and when it is diving at high speed. When soaring, the bird extends its wings, achieving increased lift, but it pulls the wings back into its body for amazing 200-mile-per-hour (320-km/h) dives. This type of wing morphing is of a much greater magnitude than the wing sweeps of the B1B and F-14, as well as the twisting wing of the experimental AAW jet.

The ability of an airplane to shape its wings in a manner similar to that of a peregrine falcon would tremendously increase efficiency and performance. Most airplanes in the military and in other applications are best suited for only one or two tasks—some soar at high altitudes, such as the spy planes, and some are capable of high-speed dives and maneuvers, such as the F-16 and F-22 fighter jets. An airplane capable of doing both, and any other kind of flight, would reduce or eliminate the huge expense of making special aircraft for special purposes. The savings would amount to billions of dollars.

Repeated, drastic alterations in the shape of a wing or another object require remarkably flexible materials. A class of material called shape-memory polymer (SMP) offers hope that researchers will discover or develop an appropriate substance. SMPs can transform from a flexible to a rigid state and back again, all under the control of stimuli such as heat, light, or electricity. In its flexible, floppy state, the material "remembers" the shape it had while rigid, and, when given a stimulus, will return to this shape. These shape changes must be performed repeatedly if they are to be useful, but not result in a weakening of the material. Although none of the SMPs of today could support a fully morphable wing, molecules exist that can stretch to twice their normal length and back again, yet offer a reasonable amount of strength. There are also special metals known as shape-memory alloys that can change on command and are stronger than polymers, although not quite as flexible.

Shape-memory alloys and polymers will play increasing roles in technology. New and improved shape-memory materials of the future may one day allow aviation engineers to design airplanes that fold and unfold their wings, yet have the agility of a hummingbird. But one of the problems of large alterations of wing shape during flight involves stability. This issue is crucial because a loss of stability during a flight, even if it is only for a moment, can result in a disastrous crash. Changing the wing from one shape to another, both of which provide stability and control, is acceptable, but there is the problem of what occurs during the transition. Think of two fishermen who are sitting in a two-seat boat, one seat at the front and one at the back. While the fishermen are sitting motionlessly the boat is stable, but if they get up and try to change seats, they may tip the boat over as they pass one another. Stability issues, as well as the development of hardy, morphable materials, are challenges that future researchers and engineers must overcome.

But people have come a long way from their past extensive use of stone, wood, and animal tissue. The right material for the job is essential, for without it very little of the technology of today, with its fast-moving jets and durable prosthetics, would be possible. Some of the most exciting scientific discoveries on the horizon will involve new and improved materials, which will allow the design and manufacture of tools and devices undreamed of today.

5

STRUCTURES

SATELLITES ARE CRITICAL for communication and navigation, but launching satellites is risky and expensive. Lifting a satellite to an altitude of 22,300 miles (35,700 km), a common orbit, requires a tremendously powerful rocket and all the equipment and technical knowledge associated with space launches. Few organizations except for the governments and militaries of large countries have the money and technical ability to do so.

But imagine a tower extending from Earth's surface up to an altitude of 62,000 miles (100,000 km). This tower, often referred to as a space elevator, would be thousands of times taller than any present structure on Earth, but it is not impossible. The great advantage of a space elevator is that it would offer an affordable alternative to expensive rocket launches. Instead of propelling a satellite into orbit on the power of rocket engine thrust, a space elevator would get a satellite in place and up to speed by using Earth's rotation and forces such as electromagnetism.

Building a tower of 62,000 miles (100,000 km) would be a daunting task. Not only are there plenty of engineering problems involving gravity and rotational acceleration, but also there is the question of what kind of material would be suitable. The stresses on a space elevator would be enormous, so the material would have to be exceptionally strong.

Although unimposing, wood cabins provided essential shelter to soldiers serving with George Washington at Valley Forge during the bitterly cold winter of 1777–78. *(Elizabeth Kirkland)*

But people have been constructing many different types of structure for thousands of years. Some of the earliest materials were wood, stone, and brick, materials that are still used today. Concrete and similar mixtures appeared later, and then, beginning in the 19th century, steel-framed buildings arose. Each of these materials has advantages, but they all have limits as well. Despite their limits, people have used them to build a wide variety of beautiful and functional structures.

Ancient Skyscrapers

The highest structure in the world for some 4,000 years was the Pyramid of Khufu (also known as the Pyramid of Cheops or the Great Pyramid of Giza), near Cairo, Egypt. Built about 4,500 years ago, the original height of this pyramidal structure was 480 feet (146 m) and it consists of more than two million blocks of stone, weighing on average about 2.5 tons (22,250 N). Most of the stones are limestone or granite.

No one knows for certain how the ancient Egyptians accomplished this monumental feat of engineering. The Pyramid of Khufu is the oldest and only remaining member of the Seven Wonders of the Ancient World, a list first compiled by ancient Greek writers. Some of the granite stones came from quarries located at a distance of about 620 miles (1,000 km), and the task of transporting these heavy blocks for such great lengths without the aid of trucks, trains, or steam-powered ships would have been exceptionally difficult. Lifting and positioning the stones to make a 480-foot (146-m) structure would also not have been easy. These ancient engineers and laborers unfortunately did not leave many written records describing their methods.

The skill of using stones or bricks as building materials is called masonry. This is an old skill, as these materials have been used for a long time. Stone was a common choice among ancient builders because it is strong and long lasting, able to withstand the onslaught of weather, chemicals, fire, and warfare. Buildings made of stone not only last a long time, but also they give the impression of permanence, which can sometimes be an important point to make. Ancient builders who constructed temples, monuments, burial markers, or other structures with a religious or civic purpose probably wanted to make sure these buildings would be around for a long time, and they also wanted to give people confidence that this would be true. Some of these structures represented religious beliefs or political concepts, and the use of long lasting stone would have inspired faith among the citizens that these ideas were enduring. Stone continues to be used today, although the impressive nature of a stone building is often mimicked in modern times with a superficial façade—for example, the front of a building may be made of cheaper, lighter ceramic material in the shape and color of stone.

Some of the most common stones for buildings are granite, marble, and limestone. Granite is often white, although it can have a number of different colors depending on its mineral content. Marble was a favored material of ancient Greek and Roman architects and artists, since this material can be brightly polished and many people find it attractive. Limestone, another attractive stone,

The state of New Hampshire contains so many granite quarries, such as this one, that it is nicknamed the "granite state." *(Elizabeth Kirkland)*

is easy to cut and shape, but it is vulnerable to chemical attack from acids, which are often released in pollution from engines and industrial factories.

The disadvantage of stone as a construction material is simple to state in terms of physics. The heaviness that gives stone its durability also means that structures made from this material cannot be very tall. Although stone is hard and strong, it weighs so much that not only is it difficult to raise to great heights, but also it must be supported by a thick base. Pyramids built by the ancient Egyptians were mostly solid, with only small tunnels and rooms in the interior. The reason is that the base had to be sturdy enough to support the stones above, so there could be few gaps or empty spaces or the structure would have collapsed under its own weight.

The same is true for brick, another durable but heavy material. Brick, a ceramic, was one of the earliest human-made construction materials, first used about 5,000 years ago. Making bricks involves mixing clay and water, which is then baked in a furnace called a kiln. The color of the resulting brick is due to the type of clay, its components, or other substances added during manufacture, as well as the baking temperature. Many bricks are red or have a reddish hue from their iron content, but almost any color is possible. The addition of copper can impart a greenish hue, for instance, and cobalt can result in blue.

Gloria Dei is one of the oldest churches in the United States. Since the founding members were Swedes, the church is sometimes called "Old Swedes." Located in Philadelphia, Pennsylvania, part of the brick structure was built in 1698–1700, with additions such as the steeple coming later. *(Kyle Kirkland)*

Bricks and stones alone will not make a sturdy structure. Mortar is a mixture of substances such as cement along with sand and water, which hardens and holds the bricks or stones in place. Walls made of bricks or stones usually have easily visible mortar, often as a thin, grayish material between layers.

The weight of stone and brick has always limited the height attainable by buildings made from these materials. The world's tallest masonry building is Philadelphia City Hall, in Philadelphia, Pennsylvania, which has a tower standing at an impressive but not overwhelming height of 548 feet (167 m). About 37 feet (11.3 m) of this height is a bronze statue of William Penn, the city's founder, perched on the top. Built from 1871 to 1901, the building itself is large and ornate—according to some critics, too ornate—with well over 600 rooms, making it one of the biggest government buildings in the world. But the tower needs walls that are 22 feet (6.7 m) thick to support its massive weight.

Making stone or brick doorways, bridges, and other spanning structures can be difficult. One of the most common methods is the arch, two types of which are shown in the figure. The weight from the bricks above compresses the lower bricks, which provide support for the upper blocks, and some of the downward force gets transmitted to the sides of the arch. The Romans used arches frequently in their aqueducts, which carried water to Rome from the outlying areas. Arches use less material than a solid wall and allow passageways underneath.

During the latter part of the Middle Ages in Europe, especially the years between 1000 and 1500, religion played a prominent role in society. People built large, beautiful churches, many of which are made of stone and are still standing today. Sturdy and majestic, some of the buildings have towers extending up to 200 feet (61 m) or more. A few of the more famous are Canterbury Cathedral in England and Notre Dame de Paris in France. Built and rebuilt over the centuries, the cathedral at Canterbury was one of the holiest sites in England, and thousands of people journeyed there every year to participate in religious ceremonies. The towers of Notre Dame de Paris rise 226 feet (69 m), one of which houses a bell weighing 28,000 pounds (124,600 N). This cathedral was the setting for French

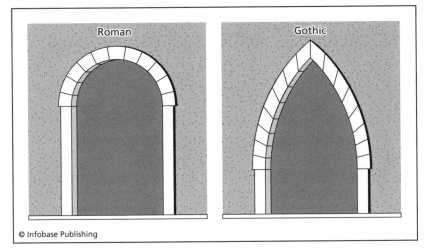

© Infobase Publishing

A Roman arch (left) is more rounded than a Gothic arch (right).

writer Victor Hugo's famous 1831 book, *The Hunchback of Notre Dame*.

Supporting the weight of these massive structures without filling up the whole interior with stone was not a simple task. The walls have to support not only their own weight but also the weight of the vault (ceiling), and since these buildings were meant to hold a large number of people, open spaces were essential. Reinforcing the walls of some of these buildings are heavy, exterior structures called buttresses, providing additional support by butting up against a wall so that it does not collapse. Flying buttresses are graceful structures that supported the walls of these massive buildings with arches, which transmitted the force of the building's weight to the ground or foundation. Reinforced with flying buttresses, the cathedral walls did not have to be solid, leaving room for large windows to let in much-needed light. The figure shows an example of a flying buttress.

Wood is another common and long-used building material. As mentioned in the previous chapter, wood is a natural composite, made from cellulose fibers and a hard substance called lignin. The fibers are generally oriented lengthwise (vertically) along the tree,

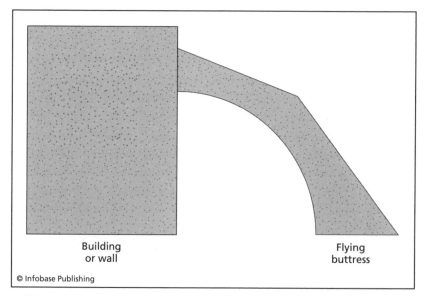

Building
or wall

Flying
buttress

© Infobase Publishing

A flying buttress provides support, "flying" from the wall and transmitting some of the burden to the ground or to the building's foundation.

giving wood a "grain" by which it is easy to split or cut. The advantages of wood over stone are that it is an easier material with which to work, yet is strong and can provide adequate support for fairly tall buildings. The disadvantages of wood include susceptibility to fire, decay, and insect damage. Wooden structures do not endure nearly as long as stone.

Even though wood is strong and not as heavy as stone, there are limits to the height and weight it can support. No one knows for sure the identity of the tallest wooden building in history, but a good candidate is a 623-foot (190-m) radio tower, now destroyed, built near Mühlacker, Germany, in the 1930s. But wood continues to be an extremely popular building material, especially to provide the frame for small, single-family houses. These structures are cheap and relatively simple to build, and they last long enough to survive for several generations.

But not all wooden structures have short lifetimes. Perhaps the most elegant wooden structures are Asian pagodas, with their curved, jutting eaves, as shown in the figure on page 110. These buildings generally served a religious function and some have survived for centuries. The tiered (layered) architecture helps make the pagoda stable during earthquakes, which are common in Japan; although the structure sways, it often will not fall down. Fire is probably the deadliest hazard to these beautiful wooden buildings.

At the early stages of construction, this house's "skeleton" is a frame made of wood. *(Kyle Kirkland)*

© Infobase Publishing

Pagodas have several layers or tiers, each with a curved projection.

Concrete and Steel

Two different building materials rose to prominence in the 19th century, offering alternatives to stone, brick, and wood. But neither of these materials was entirely new.

Both concrete and steel have their beginnings in ancient times. Concrete is a mixture of sand and gravel with cement, a substance that comes from baking lime with clay and various minerals. The addition of water causes the mixture to adhere and harden over time, forming a type of artificial, human-made stone. The Romans used concrete-like materials in structures such as bridges, but when this great civilization fell in the fifth century, the science of making concrete was lost for about 1,400 years.

Steel is a metal, an alloy that is primarily iron with a little carbon. Iron is an abundant metal but is difficult to extract and shape, because processing the metal and its ore requires temperatures of around 2,500°F (1,370°C). The process of making iron tends to add carbon, but generally too much carbon. "Pig iron" or "cast iron" can be up to 4 percent carbon, which produces a hard but brittle metal that can and often does break at inconvenient moments. (People use the name *iron* for these substances even though they contain carbon, and are not pure iron.) Most steel is less than about 1 percent carbon.

A small amount of carbon makes iron stronger because the smaller carbon atoms prevent the iron atoms in the crystals from sliding over or around each other. This makes the alloy less susceptible to bending or stretching. Iron began replacing bronze for weaponry and other applications around 1200 B.C.E., although much of this iron may not have been high quality, and the change may have been due more to the scarcity of bronze than the superiority of iron. The making of steel—as defined as an iron alloy with a low and controllable amount of carbon—did not become efficient until 1855, when British engineer Henry Bessemer (1813–98) perfected what became known as the Bessemer process. The procedure blows air through molten pig iron, igniting the carbon and burning away a desired quantity of it. When finished, this method yields a high-quality, low-carbon steel.

Steel is a strong metal that can withstand a huge amount of tensile stress. This ability to resist being stretched or torn apart makes steel a valuable material for many applications, particularly vehicles or structures subjected to strong forces such as wind or the impact of hurled projectiles. But a major disadvantage of steel is corrosion, also known as rusting. Steel contains iron, which undergoes a chemical reaction when exposed to water and air to form an oxide of iron. Rusting robs a piece of steel of its strength and gradually destroys it altogether.

Other elements besides iron and carbon can go into making steel. The addition of chromium is common, and it makes an alloy known as stainless steel. This kind of steel does not suffer as much from corrosion because the chromium forms a compound on the surface of the metal that helps protect it. Other elements are added to stainless steel and other kinds of steel to adjust their properties, making them slightly stronger or better able to resist high temperatures. These elements include nickel, titanium, copper, aluminum, and silicon.

Concrete does not suffer from corrosion, which affects most types of steel, or from rot, which affects wood. But concrete is also different from steel in that is not strong under tensile stress—even a slight bend or stretch will pull it apart. The usefulness of concrete lies instead in its great strength under the forces of compression. Concrete is a material that can support a huge amount of weight, making it ideal for the foundations of buildings.

Sometimes people use the term *cement* when referring to, say, cement sidewalks, but they are really talking about concrete. The cement, when combined with water, is the substance that forms the strong bonds holding concrete together. These bonds

Concrete is often used for a building's foundation. A house will be built on top of these concrete slabs. *(Kyle Kirkland)*

get stronger as the concrete hardens, a process called hydration because it involves water. The water not only starts the bonding process, but also it makes the material fluid and moldable. As the concrete hardens, some of the water is involved in the reactions that form the bonds, and some of the water remains behind, filling tiny spaces. If too much water remains, the concrete is seriously weakened, so concrete pourers must be careful not to add too much water to the mix.

The hardening of concrete occurs rapidly over the first few days or weeks but then slows down. Yet concrete continues to harden over time, even after a year or more. Engineers test the strength of a concrete structure after a period of 28 days, even though the material continues to harden afterward, because few people are willing to wait until the process is finally done.

As a hard, heavy material, concrete is better than wood in some ways, and worse in others. Concrete does not burn, rot, or serve as a meal to termites, and it offers better thermal insulation—it is a more effective barrier to heat, which means that a warm house stays warmer in winter and a cool house stays cooler in summer. Blocks of concrete, attached together with mortar, can make masonry structures. But wood is attractive, lightweight, and inexpensive, so even if a house's foundation is concrete, the frame is often wood.

Concrete's ability to resist compressive forces makes possible the construction of gigantic structures such as the Hoover Dam. This dam, built on the Colorado River about 30 miles (48 km) southeast of Las Vegas, Nevada, is 726.4 feet (221.5 m) tall and weighs more than 6,600,000 tons (58,740,000,000 N). Completed in 1935, there is enough concrete in this structure to pave a road 16 feet (4.9 m) wide all the way from San Francisco, California, to New York City. An average of 3,500 people per day worked on this project for five years.

The physics of concrete and steel are completely different, and for this reason the combination of the two makes a uniquely superior material. *Reinforced concrete* is concrete strengthened or reinforced with bars, usually made of steel, called rebars (**reinforcement bars**). Frenchman Jean-Louis Lambot began using reinforced concrete in the late 1840s, and much of the concrete used for structures today is of the reinforced variety.

One of the reasons the combination works so well together is that concrete provides the bulk to withstand compression while the steel rebars provide the strength to resist tension. The rebars form a kind of frame, as shown in the figure below, around which poured concrete will harden. Rebar has ridges or other protrusions on its surface so that the setting concrete hardens around these curves, locking the bar into place so that it will not easily come out. Reinforced concrete is strong and will support the weight of a tall structure, yet unlike ordinary concrete it will effectively resist stretching or bending forces that would otherwise knock it down. Both gravity and wind fail to topple it. Another reason the

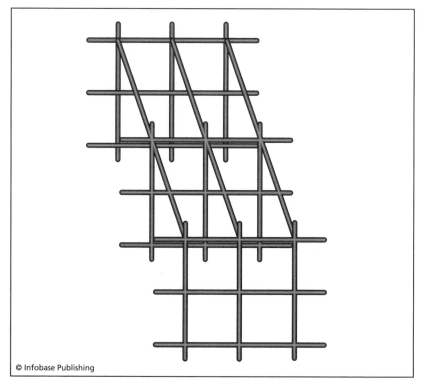

Concrete poured over steel rebar hardens and makes reinforced concrete, a material that exhibits strength under both tension and compression. This figure shows the rebars around which the concrete will harden.

combination works well is that both concrete and steel expand at about the same rate with temperature. If they did not have similar thermal expansion rates, a change in temperature would pull apart reinforced concrete since one or the other of the materials would outgrow the other.

A weakness of reinforced concrete is a susceptibility to corrosion, due to the steel content. Even though rebar is usually buried within the concrete itself, cracks and holes or contaminants can start the corrosion process and result in a serious loss of strength. One method of avoiding corrosion is to use corrosion-resistant composites instead of steel, although this elevates the cost. Other solutions involve using stainless steel or coating the rebars with a plastic material that is not subject to corrosion, which reduces or eliminates the threat.

Modern Skyscrapers

Philadelphia City Hall reaches skyward with the help of stone, and concrete supports a 961-foot (293-m) building at 311 South Wacker Drive in Chicago, but neither of these buildings towers

For many years Philadelphia's City Hall, completed in 1901, was the tallest building in the city. Although it is the tallest masonry building, City Hall is now dwarfed by the surrounding skyscrapers. *(Kyle Kirkland)*

over its city. The tallest skyscrapers of today attain their great height with steel frames. Chicago's Sears Tower is 1,451 feet (442 m) tall (the building is 1,729 feet [527 m] tall if the measurement includes the antenna system mounted on the roof), and Philadelphia's One Liberty Place rises 945 feet (288 m).

Before buildings of this size could be usefully inhabited, elevators had to be developed. Climbing the stairs to reach the 108th floor of the Sears Tower every day would get a little tiring even for the most superbly trained athlete. Although it is not a difficult task to design and make an elevator car along with a cable with which to pull it up, the earliest elevators were risky because the cable could break. People used elevators early in the 19th century to haul freight or cargo from one floor of a building to another, but they did not usually trust their safety to these devices.

Then American inventor Elisha Otis (1811–61) demonstrated his "safety elevator" to an astounded audience at an 1853 exhibition in New York. Otis's elevator had a spring to latch the elevator car into place if the hoisting rope broke. In his demonstration, Otis rode a platform to the top of an open shaft, in full sight of the audience. When he got close to the end of the lift, someone cut the rope. The audience gasped. But the car did not fall, and Otis was safe.

With elevator safety assured, buildings could expand vertically yet remain accessible. But as mentioned earlier, material such as stone or concrete that is strong enough to hold up the weight of many floors is also extremely heavy, and at some height the building would become so heavy that it could no longer support its weight. The solution was to design a "skeleton" on which to hang the walls and roof. This skeleton or frame is steel, or in a few cases, reinforced concrete.

Vertical columns are firmly rooted into the ground. Horizontal beams connect these columns at periodic intervals, holding the structure together and providing support for the floors. Sometimes builders also include diagonal beams for additional support. The horizontal and diagonal beams transmit the weight of the building to the vertical columns, which must bear the load.

In order for the columns to support this weight, they need something solid on which to rest. Hard clay will suffice for some of the smaller buildings, but the columns of the tallest skyscrapers must rest on bedrock. Rock can be found under the surface at almost any location, but the term *bedrock* generally refers to sheets or layers of solidly joined rock. This rock can support the enormous weight of a structure such as the Empire State Building without shifting or cracking.

Whether skyscrapers are possible in a given area depends on the location of the bedrock. If bedrock is only 20 to 25 feet (6.1–7.6 m) below the surface, as it is in parts of lower and midtown Manhattan in New York City, this encourages the construction of skyscrapers because builders can easily sink a concrete pillar to reach this depth. The concrete supports the vertical columns, which hold up the building. If the builder must drill to depths of 200 feet (61 m) to find bedrock, then supporting a skyscraper becomes more expensive and less reliable. The depth of bedrock has strongly influenced New York City's skyline in Manhattan, with many skyscrapers on the south end and a few more near the Empire State Building, which is between 33rd and 34th Streets, because these are places where bedrock is found close to the surface.

Since the vertical steel columns support the weight of the building, the exterior set of walls, called the curtain wall, need only hold up their own weight. These walls can therefore be almost any material, including sheets of glass or hard, transparent plastic. Such coverings give modern high-rise buildings their glinting, reflective surfaces. This is a vastly different look than the sturdy brick or concrete walls of other, smaller structures—in the buildings without steel frames to support the weight, it is the job of the walls to hold up the building, so the walls must be made of weight-bearing material such as concrete.

It is a lot easier to expand in the horizontal direction instead of vertically, and this is why most builders who want to construct large buildings spread them out over a lot of land, rather than building them up to the sky. But in places such as New York City and Hong Kong, where a huge number of organizations and

A steel frame for a skyscraper goes up in Philadelphia, Pennsylvania. This building will become the Cira Centre, as shown in the next figure. *(Kyle Kirkland)*

businesses have established themselves, there is no room to grow except upward.

Identifying the world's tallest building would seem to be a simple task requiring only a measuring tape, but it is not quite that easy. The height can be extended by antennas or other structures, which may or may not be considered a part of the building. The exact meaning of the term *building* is also relevant, for one can ask whether towers should be included if they are not meant to be occupied by people. As of April 2006, the tallest occupied building in the world is Taipei 101 in Taiwan, which stands at 1,671 feet (509 m). Taipei 101 holds this distinction even though the Sears Tower's antenna reaches 1,729 feet (527 m), and the telecommunications CN Tower in Toronto soars to 1,815 feet (553 m).

Tremendous forces experienced by these buildings do not just come from their own weight. Winds blowing against the side of the structure, or tremors from nearby earthquakes, can cause lateral (side) forces of considerable magnitude. These forces are not predictable and the building designers must calculate a worst-

The nearly finished Cira Centre is 436 feet (133 m) tall. The glass and plastic sides need not bear much weight, since the steel frame of the structure provides most of the support (see the previous figure). *(Kyle Kirkland)*

case scenario with which they believe their building may have to endure. This calculation affects all aspects of the design, such as the number and composition of the vertical columns and the connections holding them together.

Tall buildings sway in a fierce wind, and they swing like an upside-down pendulum when the ground moves during an earthquake. At least a small amount of movement will always occur in these situations, so builders must ensure that the structure remains rigid—as long as the building moves as a unit, it will not tear itself apart unless it sways too much. Strong connections among the columns and beams keep a tight grip on the whole structure. To keep a building from swaying too much, many of the tallest skyscrapers have an especially strong set of columns running through their center. This core stabilizes the building when it is subject to violent weather or ground vibrations.

A new development in stability is the tuned mass damper. A damper reduces, or dampens, an oscillation, and a mass damper does this by having a tremendous mass. An important law of motion called Newton's second law, mentioned in the previous chapter, states that the acceleration, a, of an object is directly proportional to the force, f, it experiences and inversely proportional to the object's mass, m: $a = f/m$. This law says that the greater an object's mass, the less its motion will change due to a given force— a pebble is easy to send skittering away with a swift kick, but the same kick against a massive boulder only results in a swollen toe. With a huge mass such as a gigantic concrete block at the top of a building, a system of springs or pendulums controlling the block can dampen motion by moving in opposition to the sway of the building. Engineers adjust or "tune" the mass damper specifically to reduce certain frequencies of motion to which the building is known to be vulnerable. Taipei 101 has a mass damper weighing 730 tons (6,500,000 N).

Although a lot of thought and engineering go into the design and building of skyscrapers, sometimes things go wrong. Both World Trade Center towers in New York City collapsed following the attacks of September 11, 2001, as terrorists piloted large passenger jets directly into the structures. Despite the widespread structural damage, many people were surprised the towers fell, for the builders had provided safeguards for almost every possibility, including airplane impacts. One likely reason for the collapse of the towers involves the weakening of essential columns, which was probably due to a ferocious fire caused by burning jet fuel.

Space Elevator—A Tower of the Future

The World Trade Center catastrophe showed that skyscrapers are vulnerable to attack. After watching the collapse of the towers on television, many people became uneasy about occupying tall buildings. Perhaps this event will encourage builders to more strongly consider using the horizontal rather than the vertical dimension in the future.

But there is one potential structure in which height is essential. A space elevator, mentioned at the beginning of the chapter, would need great altitude in order to fulfill its job of lifting people and objects into orbit. There is no alternative—a space elevator must reach space if it is to function.

Engineers began seriously to discuss the concept of a space elevator in the 1960s. Its primary function would be reducing the enormous expense of launching satellites and other equipment into space. Satellites perform many valuable services in communications, navigation, and science—satellites transmit conversations between people who are continents apart, provide the means by which sailors and other people find out exactly where they are and where they are headed, and offer scientists viewpoints and perspectives to study Earth that are unobtainable by anyone standing on the surface of the planet. But launching satellites into orbit is a costly endeavor, involving huge facilities and millions of dollars in equipment, in addition to the time and technical knowledge of a large staff of highly trained personnel.

A space elevator might be able to reduce launch costs by a factor of about 50. Such a reduction would open up space to even more enriching applications, and it would be so inexpensive that people could afford to take a vacation in space. It would have a tremendous impact on society and economy, and it would be a first step in humanity's colonization beyond the planet. Many people feel that colonization is essential if human civilization is to continue to grow and expand—Earth has limited room and resources, which are not enough to feed or take care of a burgeoning population.

Popular writer Arthur C. Clarke promoted the concept of a space elevator in his 1978 novel *The Fountains of Paradise*. In Clarke's book, engineers build a space elevator on the fictional island of Taprobane, which lies on the equator in the Pacific Ocean. Clarke has a splendid imagination, but he is also knowledgeable in science and engineering. People take his ideas seriously because as an author he is careful to adhere to scientific principles. In the 1940s, more than a decade before the first space launch, Clarke was one of the first people to consider the use of satellites at a geostationary orbit—an orbit of 22,300 miles (35,700 km), where satellites hover over a fixed point.

Geostationary orbit is important to satellites and would be critical for a space elevator as well. The period of an orbiting object is the time required for a single orbital revolution—one revolution around the body it is orbiting. This period depends on the satellite's altitude, and it increases with increasing altitude. At an altitude of 184 miles (296 km), the period is about 90 minutes. At 6,200 miles (10,000 km), the period is slightly less than six hours. At 62,000 miles (100,000 km), the period is almost four days.

One of the most important altitudes for satellites is the geostationary orbit of 22,300 miles (35,700 km), at which the period is 24 hours. In this orbit, satellites revolve around Earth at the same rate at which the planet rotates, so they stay over a specific point on the surface. (In practice, this requires an orbit over the equator so that the satellite's motion precisely follows Earth's surface. At any other location, the satellite's orbital revolution would not match the planet's spin.) A satellite in a geostationary orbit is like an extremely tall tower, able to exchange signals with a large area that does not change over time, since the satellite does not move relative to the surface of the planet.

The altitude of 22,300 miles (35,700 km) would also be an important one to a space elevator. Imagine a tower stretching well into the sky. As Earth rotates, the base of the tower, which is attached to the surface, must move at the same speed. The base drags the rest of the tower along with it, exerting a considerable force on the structure. A rigid tower may snap, particularly if it is very tall, and a flexible one would start to bend as the top began to lag behind the rotation.

But if the tower had its center at 22,300 miles (35,700 km)—geostationary orbit—then it would move along with the surface of Earth. The center referred to here is not necessarily the center in terms of length, but rather of mass. This is because mass plays a crucial role in all motion, as indicated by Newton's second law, described above. The center of mass of an object is its balancing point, the point at which the object balances because half its mass is on one side and half on the other. With its center of mass at a geostationary point, a space elevator would be stable.

Because the center of mass should be at 22,300 miles (35,700 km), the space elevator needs to extend well beyond this point. A lot of mass will be located at or near the base of the tower, which must support the weight of the structure. The mass above the geostationary point must equal the mass below, and a counterweight attached to the tower's peak might be necessary for stability.

Despite the problems, a space elevator is definitely possible from a physics perspective. Researchers such as David Smitherman of NASA, and scientist Bradley Edwards, whose work has been supported in part by NASA, have each drawn up designs for a space elevator. The primary goal of LiftPort, Inc., a company founded in 2003 at Bremerton, Washington, is to build a space elevator by the year 2018. These people, and others, believe not only that space elevators are possible but also that they can be built in the near future, with the potential of incredible economic benefits.

There is one overarching problem, however. Any design, drawing, blueprint, or idea, no matter how scientifically sound, involves objects that must be made of some kind of material. This material must have the properties required to perform its function. For the remarkable demands of a structure such as a space elevator, not just any material will do.

Consider concrete and steel, two of the most important structural materials in the modern world. Both of these materials are enormously strong, but they are also heavy. A tower reaching well beyond 22,300 miles (35,700 km) could not be made of either of these materials, for it would be too heavy to support its own weight. Even Kevlar, which has a tensile strength superior to steel but is much lighter, would not be able to handle the job.

Yet there are other materials, only recently discovered, that could conceivably build a space elevator. The most commonly mentioned material for such a task is made of carbon, but with a unique structure. Carbon nanotubes are extremely thin, about 20,000 times smaller in diameter than a human hair, which makes them about the size of a nanometer—0.0000000394 inches. This is where they derive part of their name, since they belong to the realm of nanotechnology, discussed in chapter 1. The bonds formed by the carbon atoms are similar to those of graphite, another material made of carbon, and the nanotube structure rolls up into a cylinder or tube. Carbon nanotubes, first discovered by Japanese physicist Sumio Iijima in 1991, have the potential to make a material with a tensile strength more than 100 times that of steel.

The great strength lies in the carbon bonds, which in carbon nanotubes are stronger than those in diamond, an amazingly hard substance also made of carbon (but with a different configuration). Molecular forces hold the cylindrical structure together. The cylinders are normally short, only about 1,000 to 10,000 times as long as they are wide. But at high pressures the nanotubes can combine, producing a ribbon or cable of various lengths.

Making carbon nanotubes is not yet an easy process, and the price of this material is high. There is nowhere near the capacity to generate the enormous amounts required by a space elevator. But Liftport, Inc., is trying to change that and has recently opened a carbon nanotube factory in Millville, New Jersey.

The space elevator cable, whether made of carbon nanotubes or some other material, will not by itself be able to lift anything. The cable will not behave like an elevator—the distances and forces are too great—it will simply be a guide. Lifting objects into space will be the job of robots, which will use treads to climb along the cable.

Even assuming that all aspects of a space elevator's design go on as planned, there are still hazards that must be considered. One important factor in any structure is the weather. Skyscrapers must withstand heavy wind, and a tower as tall as the space elevator will be subjected to the exceptionally strong winds of the upper atmosphere. But an equatorial location would be an advantage since this is a relatively quiet part of the global weather system. Wind forces can be further reduced by using thin cable, which will be permitted because the strength of carbon nanotubes guarantees sturdiness, even with only a slender ribbon. And once above the atmosphere (approximately 62 miles [100 km]), there is no more wind.

A space elevator must withstand earthquakes, storms, and ice if it is to survive, and a failure or collapse would be exceedingly expensive and dangerous. Yet with all the threats and danger, the economic and social benefits of a cable that will lead the way into space is to many people a worthwhile endeavor. Any new, enormous project involves risk and a lot of labor, as understood by people as far back as the ancient Egyptians who built the Pyramid of Khufu. Structures have risen to greater, more imposing heights since that time, as scientists and engineers developed stronger, lighter materials such as concrete and steel. With the development of even lighter, stronger materials such as carbon nanotubes, structures will continue to rise, probably all the way to the sky.

CONCLUSION

THE GOAL OF making objects that last a long time, provide the best fit, and perform the most functions is closely associated with the science of materials. Whether the material is a particle such as an atom, a fiber such as nylon, or a metal alloy such as stainless steel, its properties shape and govern the performance of any object made from it. The right material is what makes a tool, motor, or building possible.

The phase or state of matter, as discussed in chapter 2, adds variation even with the same material. Metal is much different in the solid, crystal phase than when heated to a liquid, and chapter 3 described how H_2O strongly influences all aspects of life on Earth by its existence as a gas in the atmosphere, a liquid in rivers and oceans, and a solid in icy glaciers. Transitions between states alter the structure—sometimes the change is obvious, such as the transformation from liquid water to a frozen sheet of ice, and sometimes it can be more subtle. In either case, these changes in the state of a material can have major effects on its properties, permitting the development of entirely new objects.

The 1991 movie *Terminator 2* featured a shape-changing robot of metal that could transform itself into almost any object. The robot could take the shape of a person or a helicopter, accomplishing the transformation by flowing into one or the other. Its metal was fluid, becoming solid and bonded into place only upon completion of the change.

Ordinary metal, detailed in chapter 4, does not do this. Most metals exist as solid crystals at room temperature, held together by strong metallic bonds. Heat breaks the bonds and the metal flows as a liquid if the temperature exceeds the melting point, but otherwise metal does not flow. The metal in *Terminator 2* behaves more like glass, which as mentioned in chapter 4 is generally amorphous (shapeless), lacking a crystal structure. Glass readily flows even when only slightly heated, and "solid" glass, with the absence of an internal structure, has much in common with liquids.

But an amorphous metal has been found. William Johnson, a professor at the California Institute of Technology, Atakan Peter, and their colleagues developed a metal in 1992 that solidifies without crystallizing. This metal is known as Liquidmetal alloy, and a company called Liquidmetal Technologies, in Lake Forest, California, makes and markets this product.

The glassy features of Liquidmetal make it easier than other metals to cast into shape, and it has a superior ability to retain and "remember" this shape, returning to the proper form after being stressed. Liquidmetal is easier to work with since it flows more readily, has a lower melting temperature than crystal metals, and requires less processing. Other valuable properties include resistance to corrosion and excellent strength and hardness. This material has been used to make protective casings for items such as pocket-size flash drives (storage devices for digital information).

Although the applications are limited at the present time, the uses of flowing metal, when perfected, could be enormous. Shape-changing on a scale as that in *Terminator 2* is not likely in the near future, but even minor changes in certain situations would be highly beneficial. For example, ships traveling through space at great speed must have hard armor to withstand collisions with rocks and asteroid fragments. The tremendous velocity of impact between rock and ship is capable of puncturing a wall, a disastrous event since the interior air would escape and astronauts would suffocate upon exposure to the airless vacuum of space. This would be a particularly important concern for any manned mission to

Mars, as NASA is currently planning, because the journey would take astronauts close to regions of space with a large number of asteroids. Yet even thick armor is not certain to withstand impacts, and it adds to the weight of the vehicle, increasing the cost of the mission and reducing its effectiveness.

But a glassy metal spacecraft would suffer no deadly accidents from impacts. If a hole opens, the metal flows and seals the puncture before much of the air escapes. This "self-healing" skin offers protection from damage and a safer, less bulky vehicle for the mission.

Self-healing vehicles and shape-changing structures are two of the many possible applications that future materials may fill. New materials have always resulted in the development of new and improved devices—bronze swords, glass bottles, plastic bags, jet engines, and many others. As researchers learn more about atoms, and how these atoms combine to form the millions of substances that exist on Earth and in space—and the millions more waiting to be discovered—people will gain the ability to build almost anything.

SI Units and Conversions

Unit	Quantity	Symbol	Conversion
Base Units			
meter	length	m	1 m = 3.28 feet
kilogram	mass	kg	
second	time	s	
ampere	electric current	A	
Kelvin	thermodynamic temperature	K	1 K = 1°C = 1.8°F
candela	luminous intensity	cd	
mole	amount of substance	mol	

Supplementary Units

radian	plane angle	rad	π rad = 180 degrees

Derived Units (combinations of base or supplementary units)

coulomb	electric charge	C	
cubic meter	volume	m^3	1 m^3 = 1,000 liters = 264 gallons
farad	capacitance	F	
henry	inductance	H	

Unit	Quantity	Symbol	Conversion
Derived Units (continued)			
hertz	frequency	Hz	1 Hz = 1 cycle per second
meter/second	speed	m/s	1 m/s = 2.24 miles/hour
Newton	force	N	4.4482 N = 1 pound
Ohm	electric resistance	Ω	
Pascal	pressure	Pa	101,325 Pa = 1 atmosphere
radian/second	angular speed	rad/s	π rad/s = 180 degrees/second
Tesla	magnetic flux density	T	
volt	electromotive force	V	
Watt	power	W	746 W = 1 horsepower

UNIT PREFIXES

Prefixes alter the value of the unit

Example: kilometer = 10^3 meters (1,000 meters)

Prefix	Multiplier	Symbol
femto	10^{-15}	f
pico	10^{-12}	p
nano	10^{-9}	n
micro	10^{-6}	μ
milli	10^{-3}	m
centi	10^{-2}	c
deci	10^{-1}	d
deca	10	da
hecto	10^2	h
kilo	10^3	k
mega	10^6	M
giga	10^9	G
tera	10^{12}	T

GLOSSARY

alloy   a mixture of metallic elements with other metallic or non-metallic elements

alpha particle   positively charged particles consisting of two protons and two neutrons

amorphous   without a definite shape or form

atom   a particle, consisting of a nucleus and surrounding electrons, that is the smallest part of an element that retains the element's chemical properties

brittle   easily broken or cracked

cell   in biology, the basic unit of life, consisting of nutrients and structures enveloped in a protective coating called a membrane

ceramic   a material usually made by heating or baking substances such as clay

composite   composed of fibers of one material, such as glass or carbon, embedded or glued in a matrix of another material, such as plastic

compound   made of chemical elements bonded together in specific ways

compression   the application of a force that tends to compress or squeeze a substance; opposite of tension

covalent bond   a strong chemical bond between atoms in which they share electrons

crystal   a repeating configuration of particles in a solid

deoxyribonucleic acid   DNA, an important molecule in cells that stores genetic (inherited) information

DNA   *See* DEOXYRIBONUCLEIC ACID

elasticity the ability to regain shape after becoming bent or stretched

electron a negatively charged particle, component of an atom

element a fundamental substance composed of identical atoms with characteristic properties

fluid a gas or liquid

fission breaking apart of an atomic nucleus

fusion joining of atomic nuclei to form a larger nucleus

gas a phase of matter characterized by independently moving particles; a gas always takes the form and volume of its container

grain of crystals, a unit or particle of the crystal; of wood, the orientation of fibers

hydrogen bonds forms between hydrogen and other atoms, caused by unequal sharing of electrons in covalent bonds

ionic bond a strong chemical bond held together by electrical forces

ions an electrically charged particle

isotopes atoms of an element that have the same chemical properties but differ in the composition of their nucleus, which has a varying number of neutrons

liquid a phase of matter characterized by particles that contact each other but are able to move or slide around

mass the amount of matter, which gives a body its weight on the surface of Earth

molecule a particle composed of two or more atoms

nanotechnology technology associated with small particles the size of nanometers

NASA *See* NATIONAL AERONAUTICS AND SPACE ADMINISTRATION

National Aeronautics and Space Administration the United States government agency responsible for space exploration and technology

neutron an electrically uncharged particle that, along with protons, compose atomic nuclei

nucleus the central portion of an atom, containing protons and neutrons

organic carbon-containing substances usually associated with living organisms

phase of a material, the state of its components, either a gas, liquid, solid, or plasma

plasma a phase of matter with gaseous properties but consisting of ions

plastic a material composed of polymers or polymer-like substances

polymer a chain formed by the repetitive joining or bonding of a certain type of molecule

pressure force acting on an area

protein a natural polymer found in living organisms, composed of chains of molecules known as amino acids

proton a positively charged particle that, along with neutrons, compose atomic nuclei

radioactivity emission of energy by atomic nuclei while they are undergoing transformations

reinforced concrete concrete embedded with bars, usually made of steel

shear of a force, the tendency to twist or slide

solid a phase of matter characterized by particles at fixed positions

state phase or condition of matter

strain a change in shape in response to stress

stress force per unit area acting on an object

strong force a fundamental force that holds the particles of an atom's nucleus together; also called strong nuclear force

surface tension force acting on the surface of a fluid arising from attractions among the particles

tensile strength ability to resist tension

tension the application of a force that tends to pull or stretch an object; opposite of compression

thermal pertaining to heat or temperature

viscosity a measure of a fluid's resistance to internal motion

voltage a measure of electrical force

FURTHER READING AND WEB SITES

BOOKS

Amato, Ivan. *Stuff: The Materials the World Is Made of.* New York: Basic Books, 1997. Focusing on human-made materials, this book describes the history as well as current research of the science and technology of all kinds of materials, from metal to synthetic diamonds.

Atkins, Peter. *Atkins' Molecules,* 2nd ed. Cambridge, U.K.: Cambridge University Press, 2003. Atkins, a chemist and popular science author, offers an in-depth look at a variety of important molecules, such as polymers, soaps, and the molecules underlying human senses of taste, smell, pain, and vision.

Bloomfield, Louis A. *How Things Work: The Physics of Everyday Life,* 3rd ed. New York: John Wiley & Sons, 2005. This exceptional college-level text explains the physics behind a wide variety of everyday phenomena.

Bortz, Fred. *Techno-Matter: The Materials behind the Marvels.* Fairfield, Iowa: 21st Century Books, 2001. Intended for young adults, this book explores materials science, including semiconductors, metallurgy, superconductors, and much more.

Calle, Carlos I. *Superstrings and Other Things: A Guide to Physics.* Bristol: Institute of Physics, 2001. Calle explains the laws and principles of physics in a clear and accessible manner.

Dupré, Judith and Philip Johnson. *Skyscrapers.* New York: Black Dog & Leventhal, 2001. With plenty of elegant photographs that do justice to these remarkable structures, Dupré's book describes 50 skyscrapers of the 20th century.

Gordon, J. E. *The Science of Structures and Materials.* New York: Scientific American Books, 1988. A noted materials scientist describes the scientific aspects of materials and how they are used to build structures such as bridges and airplanes.

Henderson, Harry. *Nuclear Physics.* New York: Facts On File, 1998. Telling the story of the development of nuclear physics from a broad perspective, this book focuses on the work of Marie and Pierre Curie, Ernest Rutherford, Neils Bohr, Lise Meitner, Richard Feynman, and Murray Gell-Mann.

Suplee, Curt. *The New Everyday Science Explained.* Washington, D.C.: National Geographic Society, 2004. This richly illustrated book provides concise scientific answers to some of the most basic questions about people and nature.

Tweed, Mark. *Essential Elements: Atoms, Quarks, and the Periodic Table.* New York: Walker & Company, 2003. This small volume provides a concise and readable introduction to the components of the atom and the properties of the fundamental elements.

WEB SITES

American Institute of Physics. "Physics Success Stories." Available online. URL: http://www.aip.org/success/. Accessed on August 25, 2006. Examples of how the study of physics has impacted society and technology.

American Physical Society. "Physics Central." Available online. URL: http://www.physicscentral.com/. Accessed on August 25, 2006. A collection of articles, illustrations, and photographs explaining physics and its applications, and introducing some of the physicists who are advancing the frontiers of physics even farther.

Chaplin, Martin. "Water Structure and Behavior." Available online. URL: http://www.lsbu.ac.uk/water/index2.html. Accessed on August 25, 2006. This Web site contains a huge amount of information on the water molecule and its properties and interactions, and the reasons water so strongly affects human health and welfare.

Day, Dwayne A. "Composites and Advanced Materials." Available online. URL: http://www.centennialofflight.gov/essay/Evolution_of_Technology/composites/Tech40.htm. Accessed on August 25, 2006. This Web page discusses the importance of composites and other materials in the development of modern aircraft.

Eastman, Timothy E. "Perspectives on Plasma—the Fourth State of Matter." Available online. URL: http://www.plasmas.org/. Accessed on August 25, 2006. Tutorials covering the basic concepts and applications of plasmas.

Exploratorium: The Museum of Science, Art and Human Perception. Available online. URL: http://www.exploratorium. edu/. Accessed on August 25, 2006. An excellent Web resource containing much information on the scientific explanations of everyday things.

Foresight Institute homepage. Available online. URL: http://www. foresight.org/. Accessed on August 25, 2006. Foresight is a nonprofit organization dedicated to promoting nanotechnology applications and advancing public awareness of this promising technology. Their Web pages offer news, information, and links to other nanotechnology Web sites.

HowStuffWorks, Inc., homepage. Available online. URL: http:// www.howstuffworks.com/. Accessed on August 25, 2006. Contains a large number of articles, generally written by knowledgeable authors, explaining the science behind everything from computers to satellites.

Lawrence Berkeley National Laboratory. "Exploring the Material World." Available online. URL: http://www.lbl.gov/MicroWorlds/module_index.html. Accessed on August 25, 2006. Teaching modules on this Web site include "Exploring the Material World," "Kevlar—the Wonder Material," and "Selenium: A Window on the Wetlands."

LiftPort Group homepage. Available online. URL: http://www.lift-port.com/. Accessed on August 25, 2006. News and information from the corporation that hopes to build a space elevator by 2018.

Nave, Carl R. "HyperPhysics Concepts." Available online. URL: http://hyperphysics.phy-astr.gsu.edu/hbase/hph.html. Accessed on August 25, 2006. This comprehensive resource for students offers illustrated explanations and examples of the basic concepts of physics, including condensed matter.

Nuclear Energy Institute (NEI) homepage. Available online. URL: http://www.nei.org/. Accessed on August 25, 2006. NEI members include companies involved in the maintenance and operation of nuclear power plants, and companies involved in the field of nuclear medicine. This institute helps set policies affecting the industry, and its Web page includes news and basic information on all aspects of nuclear energy.

Portland Cement Association. "Effect of Cement Characteristics on Concrete Properties." Available online. URL: http://www.cement.org/tech/cct_cement_characteristics.asp. Accessed on August 25, 2006. This Web page discusses properties of cement that are crucial in the formation of concrete.

PERIODIC TABLE OF THE ELEMENTS

Key: atomic number — symbol — atomic weight

3 Li 6.941

1 IA	2 IIA	3 IIIB	4 IVB	5 VB	6 VIB	7 VIIB	8 VIIIB	9 VIIIB	10 VIIIB	11 IB	12 IIB	13 IIIA	14 IVA	15 VA	16 VIA	17 VIIA	18 VIIIA
1 H 1.00794																	2 He 4.0026
3 Li 6.941	4 Be 9.0122											5 B 10.81	6 C 12.011	7 N 14.0067	8 O 15.9994	9 F 18.9984	10 Ne 20.1798
11 Na 22.9898	12 Mg 24.3051											13 Al 26.9815	14 Si 28.0855	15 P 30.9738	16 S 32.067	17 Cl 35.4528	18 Ar 39.948
19 K 39.0938	20 Ca 40.078	21 Sc 44.9559	22 Ti 47.867	23 V 50.9415	24 Cr 51.9962	25 Mn 54.938	26 Fe 55.845	27 Co 58.9332	28 Ni 58.6934	29 Cu 63.546	30 Zn 65.409	31 Ga 69.723	32 Ge 72.61	33 As 74.9216	34 Se 78.96	35 Br 79.904	36 Kr 83.798
37 Rb 85.4678	38 Sr 87.62	39 Y 88.906	40 Zr 91.224	41 Nb 92.9064	42 Mo 95.94	43 Tc (98)	44 Ru 101.07	45 Rh 102.9055	46 Pd 106.42	47 Ag 107.8682	48 Cd 112.412	49 In 114.818	50 Sn 118.711	51 Sb 121.760	52 Te 127.60	53 I 126.9045	54 Xe 131.29
55 Cs 132.9054	56 Ba 137.328	57–70 ☆	72 Hf 178.49	73 Ta 180.948	74 W 183.84	75 Re 186.207	76 Os 190.23	77 Ir 192.217	78 Pt 195.08	79 Au 196.9655	80 Hg 200.59	81 Tl 204.3833	82 Pb 207.2	83 Bi 208.9804	84 Po (209)	85 At (210)	86 Rn (222)
87 Fr (223)	88 Ra (226)	89–102 ★	104 Rf (261)	105 Db (262)	106 Sg (266)	107 Bh (262)	108 Hs (263)	109 Mt (268)	110 Ds (271)	111 Rg (272)	112 Uub (277)	113 Uut (284)	114 Uuq (285)	115 Uup (288)	116 Uuh (292)		

☆ lanthanoids

57 La 138.9055	58 Ce 140.115	59 Pr 140.908	60 Nd 144.24	61 Pm (145)	62 Sm 150.36	63 Eu 151.966	64 Gd 157.25	65 Tb 158.9253	66 Dy 162.500	67 Ho 164.9303	68 Er 167.26	69 Tm 168.9342	70 Yb 173.04	71 Lu 174.967

★ actinoids

89 Ac (227)	90 Th 232.0381	91 Pa 231.036	92 U 238.0289	93 Np (237)	94 Pu (244)	95 Am 243	96 Cm (247)	97 Bk (247)	98 Cf (251)	99 Es (252)	100 Fm (257)	101 Md (258)	102 No (259)	103 Lr (260)

numbers in parentheses are atomic mass numbers of most stable isotopes

THE CHEMICAL ELEMENTS

(g) none (c) non-metallics

element	symbol	a.n.
carbon	C	6
hydrogen	H	1

(g) chalcogen (c) non-metallics

element	symbol	a.n.
oxygen	O	8
polonium	Po	84
selenium	Se	34
sulfur	S	16
tellurium	Te	52
ununhexium	Uuh	116

(g) alkali metal (c) metallics

element	symbol	a.n.
cesium	Cs	55
francium	Fr	87
lithium	Li	3
potassium	K	19
rubidium	Rb	37
sodium	Na	11

(g) alkaline earth metal (c) metallics

element	symbol	a.n.
barium	Ba	56
beryllium	Be	4
calcium	Ca	20
magnesium	Mg	12
radium	Ra	88
strontium	Sr	38

(g) none (c) metallics

element	symbol	a.n.	element	symbol	a.n.
aluminum	Al	13	scandium	Sc	21
bohrium	Bh	107	seaborgium	Sg	106
cadmium	Cd	48	silver	Ag***	47
chromium	Cr	24	tantalum	Ta	73
cobalt	Co	27	technetium	Tc	43
copper	Cu***	29	thallium	Tl	81
darmstadtium	Ds	110	titanium	Ti	22
dubnium	Db	105	tin	Sn	50
gallium	Ga	31	tungsten	W	74
gold	Au***	79	ununbium	Uub	112
hafnium	Hf	72	ununtrium	Uut	113
hassium	Hs	108	ununquadium	Uuq	114
indium	In	49	vanadium	V	23
iridium	Ir****	77	yttrium	Y	39
iron	Fe	26	zinc	Zn	30
lawrencium	Lr	103	zirconium	Zr	40
lead	Pb	82			
lutetium	Lu	71			
manganese	Mn	25			
meitnerium	Mt	109			
mercury	Hg	80			
molybdenum	Mo	42			
nickel	Ni	28			
niobium	Nb	41			
osmium	Os****	76			
palladium	Pd****	46			
platinum	Pt****	78			
rhenium	Re	75			
rhodium	Rh****	45			
roentgenium	Rg	111			
ruthenium	Ru****	44			
rutherfordium	Rf	104			

(g) pnictogen (c) metallics

element	symbol	a.n.
arsenic	As*	33
antimony	Sb*	51
bismuth	Bi	83
nitrogen	N	7
phosphorus	P**	15
ununpentium	Uup	115

(g) none (c) semi-metallics

element	symbol	a.n.
boron	B	5
germanium	Ge	32
silicon	Si	14

(g) actinoid (c) metallics

element	symbol	a.n.
actinium	Ac	89
americium	Am	95
berkelium	Bk	97
californium	Cf	98
curium	Cm	96
einsteinium	Es	99
fermium	Fm	100
mendelevium	Md	101
neptunium	Np	93
nobelium	No	102
plutonium	Pu	94
protactinium	Pa	91
thorium	Th	90
uranium	U	92

(g) halogens (c) non-metallics

element	symbol	a.n.
astatine	At*	85
bromine	Br	35
chlorine	Cl	17
fluorine	F	9
iodine	I	53

(g) lanthanoid (c) metallics

element	symbol	a.n.
cerium	Ce	58
dysprosium	Dy	66
erbium	Er	68
europium	Eu	63
gadolinium	Gd	64
holmium	Ho	67
lanthanum	La	57
neodymium	Nd	60
praseodymium	Pr	59
promethium	Pm	61
samarium	Sm	62
terbium	Tb	65
thulium	Tm	69
ytterbium	Yb	70

(g) noble gases (c) non-metallics

element	symbol	a.n.
argon	Ar	18
helium	He	2
krypton	Kr	36
neon	Ne	10
radon	Rn	86
xenon	Xe	54

* = semi-metallics (c)
** = non-metallics (c)
*** = coinage metal (g)
**** = precious metal (g)

a.n. = atomic number
(g) = group
(c) = classification

INDEX